THE PLAGUE

Fiction and Resistance

TWAYNE'S MASTERWORK STUDIES

Robert Lecker, General Editor

THE PLAGUE

Fiction and Resistance

Steven G. Kellman

TWAYNE PUBLISHERS • NEW YORK
Maxwell Macmillan Canada • Toronto
Maxwell Macmillan International • New York Oxford Singapore Sydney

Twayne's Masterwork Studies No. 110

The Plague: Fiction and Resistance
Steven G. Kellman

Twayne Publishers
Macmillan Publishing Company
866 Third Avenue
New York, New York 10022

Maxwell Macmillan Canada, Inc.
1200 Eglinton Avenue East
Suite 200
Don Mills, Ontario M3C 3N1

Library of Congress Cataloging-in-Publication Data
Kellman, Steven G., 1947–
    The plague : fiction and resistance / Steven G. Kellman.
        p.   cm.—(Twayne's masterwork studies ; no. 110)
    Includes bibliographical references and index.
    ISBN 0-8057-8361-X.—ISBN 0-8057-8575-2 (pbk.)
    3. Plague in literature. I. Title. II. Series.
PQ2605.A3734P436   1993
843'.914—dc20   92-28710
                                                 CIP

The paper used in this publication meets the minimum requirements of American National Standard for Information Sciences—Permanence of Paper for Printed Library Materials. ANSI Z3948-1984.∞™

10 9 8 7 6 5 4 3 2 1 (hc)
10 9 8 7 6 5 4 3 2 1 (pb)

Printed in the United States of America

CONTENTS

Chez M.? Vincent proche S.º Benoit rüe S.ᵗ Jacques. à Paris

Plague (from the *Five Deaths*), c. 1648, Stefano della Bella
(Italian, 1610–1664)
Philadelphia Museum of Art: SmithKline Corporation Collection

NOTE ON THE REFERENCES
AND ACKNOWLEDGMENTS

Quotations from *The Plague* are from the Stuart Gilbert translation published in 1948 by Alfred A. Knopf, the only published English translation. Page references, cited in parentheses, are to the Modern Library college edition, either hardcover or paperback. Random House, which now owns Knopf, has also published the Gilbert translation in a Vintage Books paperback. The text of the two formats is identical except that the pagination is slightly different and the Vintage edition unaccountably omits the epigraph by Daniel Defoe. Occasional references to the original text of *La Peste* are to the definitive Pléiade edition published by Gallimard in 1962 as part of the first volume of Camus's collected works.

I have taught the book to students at a variety of levels, institutions, and locales over the past two decades and am endebted to them for mutual discoveries. Starting the novel again with each successive class has not been exactly the same as rolling a boulder from the bottom of a mountain. I am also grateful for lively discussions of plagues and praxis with Carolyn Nizzi Warmbold, a grand scholar whose own efforts against a nonallegorical epidemic deserve hats off.

CHRONOLOGY:
ALBERT CAMUS'S LIFE AND WORKS

More than most other authors, Camus rooted his writings in the great public events of his time, including World War II, the cold war, and the Algerian war. As an actor, playwright, and journalist, as well as novelist and essayist, he was a prominent figure in European intellectual life for three decades. This chronology attempts to place Camus's career as a writer within the context of the political and cultural history that helped shape him and that he helped shape.

1913	Albert Camus born 7 November in Mondovi, a village in the interior of Algeria, then administered as part of France. Second son of Lucien Auguste Camus, a winery worker whose grandparents had emigrated from Bordeaux soon after France conquered Algeria in 1830, and of Catherine Sintès, whose grandparents had come from the Spanish island of Minorca. Future author's mother cannot read or write.
1914	Assassination of Archduke Francis Ferdinand on 28 June triggers World War I. Camus's father mobilized in the First Regiment of Zouaves, North African troops. His mother takes the family to Belcourt, a working-class district of Algiers, where they stay with her mother, Marie Catherine (Cardona) Sintès. In September, father wounded in the First Battle of the Marne; dies 11 October.
1914–1920	Camus's mother, who suffered an attack that has left her partially deaf and with a speech impairment, works in a munitions factory and then as a cleaning woman. She, her mother, her brothers Etienne and Joseph Sintès, Albert, and his older brother Lucien (born 1910) live in a three-room apartment without electricity or running water, sharing a toilet with two other apartments.
1918–1923	Primary school teacher Louis Germain, to whom Camus will later dedicate his Nobel Prize speeches, takes an interest in

young Albert, provides him with extra instruction, and enters him into competition for scholarships to secondary school.

1923–1932   On a scholarship, Camus is a day-boarder at the Lycée Bugeaud in Algiers. Teacher Jean Grenier, who will develop into a lifelong friend, becomes his mentor. Camus becomes interested in sports; plays goalie position on soccer team.

1930   Shows first symptoms of tuberculosis. To deal with the disease, leaves the family apartment and moves in with his uncle Gustave Acault, a butcher and a Voltairean anarchist. Through his uncle, discovers Gide, Malraux, and Montherlant. Grandmother Sintès dies. Later he will be hospitalized for pneumothorax treatment and then will live independently, in the four corners of Algiers, alone or with others.

1930–1936   Studies philosophy at the University of Algiers, financed in part by loans and by odd jobs, including auto accessory sales, clerkship with city administration, and research staff of university's meteorological service.

1932   Studies philosophy under Grenier. Publishes four articles in Algerian journal *Sud*.

1933   Hitler becomes chancellor of Germany. Camus participates in antifascist movement. At Grenier's suggestion, reads Proust.

1934   Marries fellow student Simone Hié 16 June. They are supported by Simone's physician mother and by Camus's assorted jobs, including clerk for shipping company and for driver's license bureau. Joins Communist party; assigned to propaganda work among the Muslim populations. Exempted from military service because of lungs.

1935   Travels to Majorca. Works on first book, essays and sketches to be called *L'Envers et l'endroit* (The Wrong Side and the Right Side).

1936   Completes diploma thesis on the relationships between Hellenism and Christianity in Plotinus and Saint Augustine. Reads Epictetus, Pascal, Kierkegaard, Malraux, Gide. Poor health rules out teaching career. Travels in Central Europe, during which marriage to Simone breaks up. Cofounds Théâtre du Travail after taking over Maison de la Culture with friends. Collaborates in writing play *Révolte dans les Asturies* (Revolt in the Asturias), which is banned for performance but published. Leftist coalition Popular Front wins French elections. Spanish Civil War starts in July.

1936–1937   As actor for Radio Algiers, tours cities and villages of Algeria.

Chronology

1937   Becomes journalist for new liberal newspaper *Alger-Républicain*. At Maison de la Culture lectures on "the new Mediterranean culture." Expelled from Communist party because insists on continuing anticolonialist campaigns among Muslims. *L'Envers et l'endroit* published in May. Travels in France and Italy. Works on *La Mort heureuse* (A Happy Death). Works in Théâtre de l'Equipe, which replaces disbanded Théâtre du Travail.

1938   Reviews Sartre's *La Nausée* (Nausea). Reads Nietzsche and Kierkegaard. Writing what will become *Caligula*, *L'Etranger* (The Stranger), and *Le Mythe de Sisyphe* (The Myth of Sisyphus). Collapse of Popular Front. Munich Pact signed to appease Hitler on 30 September.

1939   Reading Epicurus and the Stoics. With Gabriel Audisio, Emmanuel Roblès, and others, founds the review *Rivages*. *Noces* (Nuptials) published in May. Reports on famine in Kabyle for *Alger-Républicain*. Czechoslovakia annexed by Germans. Germany invades Poland 1 September. France declares war 3 September. Camus attempts to enlist but rejected because of health. *Alger-Républicain* ceases publication. Camus visits Oran.

1940   Moves to Paris to work on layout for *Paris-Soir*. Completes *L'Etranger*. Germans invade France 10 May. France surrenders 22 June. Profascist Pétain administration governs southern France out of Vichy, while Germans occupy the North. Camus moves south with staff of *Paris-Soir* but leaves job in December. Marries Francine Faure, math teacher from Oran whom he had met in Algiers in 1937, on 3 December.

1941   Returns to Oran, where he teaches at private school attended by many Jewish children. Completes *Le Mythe de Sisyphe*. Works on *La Peste* (The Plague). Reads Melville, Tolstoy, Marcus Aurelius, Vigny, Sade.

1942   To recover from tuberculosis attack, goes with Francine to Chambon-sur-Lignon, in mountains of central France. Francine returns to Oran, and after Allied landing in North Africa, Camus becomes separated from her until the Liberation. Joins Resistance network of underground newspaper *Combat* in Lyons region. *L'Etranger* published in July. Reading Defoe, Cervantes, Balzac, Madame de Lafayette, Kierkegaard, Spinoza. *Le Mythe de Sisyphe* published in December.

1943   Works on *Le Malentendu* (The Misunderstanding) and *Lettre à un ami allemand* (Letter to a German Friend). Moves to

Paris, where he joins the editorial staff of Gallimard and works on *Combat*.

1944   Meets Sartre and other influential intellectuals. Paris liberated on 24 August. Becomes editor of *Combat*. *Le Malentendu* produced.

1945   Armistice in Europe on 8 May. Visits Algeria to report on massacres by colonial government. Atomic bomb dropped on Hiroshima on 6 August. Becomes father of twins, Jean and Catherine, on 5 September. *Caligula* produced. *Lettres à un ami allemand* published. France becoming embroiled in war with nationalists in Indochina.

1946   Visits the United States. Completes *La Peste*. Discovers writings of Simone Weil, which will be published under his editorship by Gallimard. Begins close friendship with poet René Char. Nuremburg trials lead to conviction and execution of Nazi war criminals. New French constitution creates Fourth Republic.

1947   Protests French repression of revolt in Madagascar. *La Peste* published in June, to great success. Leaves financially troubled *Combat*. His political polemics lead to break with Maurice Merleau-Ponty. Marshall Plan for reconstruction of Europe implemented.

1948   Czech Communist coup d'état in Prague. Camus visits Algeria. Berlin blockade in July. *L'Etat de siège* (State of Siege), written in collaboration with actor-director Jean-Louis Barrault, unsuccessfully produced 27 October.

1949   Makes appeal on behalf of Greek Communists who are sentenced to death. From June through August, makes lecture tour of South America, during which his health deteriorates. *Les Justes* (The Just Assassins) produced 15 December.

1950   *Actuelles I*, a collection of mostly journalistic prose pieces from 1944–48, published. Korean War begins when North Korean troops invade South and United Nations forces, primarily American, are sent in response.

1951   *L'Homme révolté* (The Rebel) published in October; provokes heated and sustained controversy leading to Camus's break with Sartre and other Marxists. Through written deposition, Camus testifies in a trial of Algerian nationalists in December.

1952   Visits Algeria. Public break with Sartre in August. Works on *Le Premier Homme* (The First Man), a novel; *L'Exil et le royaume* (Exile and the Kingdom), short fiction; and *Don Juan*, a play.

Chronology

1953   Speaks out against action by Soviet troops to crush East Berlin riots. *Actuelles II*, prose pieces from 1948–53, published in June. Armistice in Korea in July. Becomes director of Festival of Angers; stages his own adaptations of works by Pedro Calderòn and Pierre de Larivey.

1954   *L'Eté* (Summer), prose pieces from 1939–53, published March. Travels in Italy in November. Doing no writing and, except for an appeal on behalf of seven Tunisians sentenced to death, engaging in minimal political activity. Battle of Dien Bien Phu ends French control in Southeast Asia. Nasser becomes premier of Egypt. Riots in Morocco; independence movements growing throughout North Africa. Algerian Muslims begin armed revolt against France in November, initiating cycle of violence and reprisals.

1955   Camus's adaptation of Dino Buzzati's *Un Cas intéressant* (An Interesting Case) is staged. Travels in Greece. Returns to journalism as contributor to *L'Express*; supports election of Pierre Mendès-France and writes about the Algerian problem. Rebuffed in his appeals for both sides of the Algerian war to respect civilians and for a truce.

1956   *La Chute* (The Fall) published in May. Camus's adaptation of Faulkner's *Requiem for a Nun* staged in September. France, United Kingdom, and Israel seize Suez but withdraw. Camus protests Soviet suppression of Hungarian revolution.

1957   *L'Exil et le royaume* published in March. Camus's adaptation of Lope de Vega's *Chevalier d'Olmédo* staged at Festival of Angers. "Réflexions sur la guillotine" (Reflections on the Guillotine) published in a volume containing other attacks on capital punishment by Arthur Koestler and Jean Bloch-Michel. On 17 October, Camus becomes the ninth Frenchman and second youngest author to be awarded the Nobel Prize for Literature.

1958   In ill health. *Actuelles III*, articles on Algeria from 1939–58, published in June but generally ignored. Travels in Greece. Increased terrorism and repression in Algeria. Charles de Gaulle returns to head French government.

1959   Camus's adaptation of Dostoyevski's *The Possessed* staged. Works on *Le Premier Homme* (never completed).

1960   On 4 January, killed instantaneously when car driven by Michel Gallimard crashes into a tree near the French village of Villeblevin.

LITERARY AND HISTORICAL CONTEXT

The Plague (from *On Death, Part II*), 1898–1909, Max Klinger
(German, 1857–1920)
Philadelphia Museum of Art: SmithKline Corporation Collection

1

Zeitgeist and Angst

Though it lacks a single bomber, battleship, or hand grenade, *The Plague* is as much a product of World War II as *The Naked and the Dead* and *From Here to Eternity*. Albert Camus began writing *The Plague* during the year following the German defeat of France, and he completed his manuscript during the year following the Liberation. In statements made in the years after its publication, Camus confirmed what was clear to many contemporary French readers: that, though set in Algeria sometime during the fifth decade of the twentieth century, *The Plague* is, among much else, a disguised account of the European struggle against fascism.

When Germany invaded Poland on 1 September 1939, France and Britain were bound by treaties to oppose it. Neither, however, was prepared for the military might of the Nazi aggressor, and following six months of indecisive posturing and six weeks of actual fighting on their own soil, the French forces were routed. After surrendering to Germany on 22 June 1940, France was split into two zones. The North was occupied and administered by the German invader, while the South was governed by the collaborationist regime of Marshal Henri Philippe Pétain, who had been a French hero of World War I. For all but a few months, most of the French experienced World War II as captives rather than belligerents. Like the people of Oran during the plague, they were effectually quarantined from the outside world, forced to come to terms one way or another with the grim realities of isolation and privation.

Camus's personal situation during the composition of *The Plague* paralleled that of the novel's characters and of many of his fellow French citizens. At the time of the Allied landing in North Africa, Camus was in the mountains of central France recuperating from another attack of tuberculosis. His wife Francine had returned home to Oran, and for the duration of the war Camus was unable to leave France or rejoin his wife. Because of the movement of Axis and Allied forces, Camus wrote most of his second novel in a situation of enforced separation and hardship not unlike that of the Oranians in *The Plague*.

Upon its publication, in 1947, the novel was widely regarded and admired as a crucial expression of existentialism, a philosophical movement that was extremely popular in the decade or so following World War II. Based in the Left Bank of Paris, where it was championed by Jean-Paul Sartre, Simone de Beauvoir, and Maurice Merleau-Ponty, existentialism had its roots in the writings of recent German philosophers, particularly Edmund Husserl, Karl Jaspers, and Martin Heidegger, though its legacy can be traced back through Friedrich Nietzsche and Søren Kierkegaard as far as the pre-Socratic Greek Heraclitus. Never a systematic philosophy, existentialism was, in fact, a product of skepticism toward the intellectual arrogance of rational systems. So fashionable was the term existentialism for most of two decades that it became a convenient catchall for a variety of attitudes, beliefs, and moods shared by a youthful, disillusioned generation in Western Europe and North America. Existentialism was the embodiment of a postwar zeitgeist profoundly cynical toward the shibboleths and values that had facilitated and camouflaged global catastrophe. It insisted that existence precedes essence, that nothing is given, nothingness is the given. In the vast, indifferent universe in which we live but are never at home, the individual is ineluctably responsible for creating his or her own identity. Five A's—*alienation, absurdity, angst, anomie,* and *anxiety*—seemed indispensable to the vocabulary of anyone who aspired to speak the language of existentialism, and there were many.

For a while, particularly in philosophical writings like *The Myth of Sisyphus*, Camus was a very prominent existentialist. The Algerian newcomer, whom Sartre later, in his obituary, called a "Cartesian of the absurd" became a frequent companion of Sartre and Beauvoir during the heady days following liberation in Paris. Camus became increasingly uncomfortable, however, in the role of high priest of the new cult of the posthumous God. Rejecting the faddishness of it all, he began insisting on significant differences between his ideas and those of Sartre, and he maintained to interviewers that he was not an existentialist. Following their feud in 1951, he no longer even called himself a friend of Sartre's.

Nevertheless, whether or not it is technically existentialist, and whether or not the term has through overuse ceased to have any clear definition, *The Plague* is very much an embodiment of the attitudes of many Europeans at the middle of the twentieth century. Behind this novel that insists on being a chronicle, that is tolerant of everything but falsehood, lies widespread disappointment and even bitterness in the failure of the international crusade to preserve democracy during the Spanish Civil War of 1936–39. The destruction of the Spanish Republic was followed, a year later, by the fall of the Third Republic in France. Even before the German invasion, a succession of indecisive, undistinguished coalition governments had been weakened by scandal and by public doubt over the integrity and honesty of the politicians who formed them. During the first six months of official belligerency between Germany and France, feckless French leaders did little more than mobilize troops and issue pious proclamations. It was a phase that came to be known by the phrase "the phony war," and the actual war that followed was brief, brutal, and, for France, catastrophic. The porousness of the supposedly impregnable Maginot Line signified not only military vulnerability but a fundamental failure of candor and will.

"Phony" is Holden Caulfield's favorite term of derision in J. D. Salinger's *The Catcher in the Rye*, published in 1951, four years after

Camus's *The Plague*. Though one is a hospitalized adolescent and the other is a 35-year-old physician, the narrators of both books have almost no patience for vacuous rhetoric. Both books are reactions against the moral bankruptcy of a society based on deceit. Camus's Dr. Rieux cannot abide a lie, whether in the florid prose he fears from the journalist Raymond Rambert or in his own austere attempts to recount the ordeal of Oran. It is necessary, he reminds the reader more than once, to state that two plus two equals four, and nothing more. After Auschwitz and Hiroshima, the use of language for anything but the truth seems frivolous and even criminal.

While *The Catcher in the Rye* develops the distinctively American theme of an individual renegade against community norms, *The Plague* is more centrally concerned with collective responsibilities, with human beings as social creatures. If Salinger extends the tradition of Henry David Thoreau serenely alone at Walden Pond or claustrophobic Huck Finn lighting out for the territory ahead, *The Plague* bears the legacy of European thinkers who address the role of the individual *within* society. More specifically, the book appeared in the aftermath of the most devastating challenge to its assumptions and continuity that Western European civilization had yet experienced. *The Plague* is one honest author's response to the unprecedented horrors of World War II. Behind Rieux's act of witness to the epidemic and quarantine in a fictional Oran lies the experience of political betrayal, exile, oppression, and mass murder that Camus, an Algerian *pied-noir* (literally, black foot) trapped in France during its years of greatest gloom, knew only too well.

The most important issues for Camus's pestilence-ridden populace are less medical than they are ethical. How does one behave in a time of plague? Following Nietzsche's obituary proclamation that "God is dead," Camus could not assume any absolute, divinely sanctioned code of conduct. His characters, like those of Sartre and Beauvoir, find themselves situated in a rather inhospitable universe whose details seem gratuitous, contingent, lacking the substance of necessary design—in a word, *absurd*. Like the people of France who suddenly faced the daily realities of oppression and mass murder, Rieux, Tarrou, Rambert, Grand, Cottard, Paneloux, and the others must devise strategies to cope with the evil of an implacable disease that is devastating their community. Some, like those in the French Resistance that Camus himself joined, choose to struggle against the enemy, though victory is far from certain and their own efforts might even be counterproductive; in occupied France, at least, the Germans retaliated against underground sabotage by taking the lives of innocent hostages. Others, like Pétain and many more French than wanted to admit it following the Liberation, collude with evil; they find the epidemic in Oran a signal opportunity for personal profit. The difficult moral choices posed by the Occupation and embodied by *The Plague* continued to echo throughout French culture in the war crimes tribunals, for Klaus Barbie and others, that decades after the conclusion of World War II forced the nation to recall and confront the question of what to do and not to do in a time of plague.

Writers are, willy-nilly, the products of the time and place in which they live. But they are also, by the mere fact of being writers rather than miners or accountants, anomalies, atypical of the world on which they draw. More than most other authors, Camus, a child of the Algerian proletariat living among the Parisian intelligentsia and writing about human alienation, stood both inside and outside history. *The Plague* is a document of moral anguish in the midtwentieth century, and its power and authority come precisely from its own discomfort with the times. Over the years, Camus's reputation has fluctuated in France, but an American critic, Robert Greer Cohn, follows many others in judging his work both timely and timeless: "[A]ll in all, including the sensitivity, the courage, the lucidity, the culture, the style, the sense of humor, he was probably what we Americans all along tended to think he was: beyond all intellectual fashions and ideological factions, the finest, most authentic voice of his age."[1]

2

The Importance of the Work

I was born in 1947, five months after *La Peste*—translated the following year as *The Plague*—was published. And for many of my generation, Camus's novel, like *The Catcher in the Rye*, Golding's *Lord of the Flies* (1954), and Heller's *Catch-22*, (1961), was a book that we devoured although, and because, it was not assigned in school. Along with his ally and adversary Jean-Paul Sartre, Albert Camus embodied exactly the kind of author whom ambitious literary adolescents might admire: neither a hack nor a harlequin, someone for whom writing is an extension of thinking (the only worthwhile thinking being honest confrontation with fundamental questions of personal, social, and cosmic identity). "A novel," wrote Camus in his review of Jean-Paul Sartre's 1938 novel *Nausea*, "is never anything but a philosophy expressed in images."[1] A glance at any list of best-selling novels will quickly confirm the fallacy of that remark. But for those of us enamored of both philosophy and literature and loath to choose between truth and beauty, *The Plague* seemed a fortunate fusion. Yes, it was a story, but in reading it we had the sense of grappling with vital questions about what used to be called "the human condition."

The Importance of the Work

A 1983 survey of American graduate schools revealed that *The Plague* was on the required reading list in 46.7 percent of M.A. programs in French and 53.8 percent of Ph.D. programs.[2] But the novel has become the common cultural equipment for more than just specialists in French literature; it is frequently found on undergraduate syllabi for courses under a wide variety of rubrics—English, philosophy, humanities, history, political science, even medicine. When, in the spring of 1989, the University of North Carolina at Greensboro organized its first "All-College Read," *The Plague* was the favorite—easily outpolling Mary Shelley's *Frankenstein* (1818) by two to one—for a text on which 3,000 students and 300 faculty from throughout the College of Arts and Sciences would converge. Volunteers took turns in a marathon public reading of *The Plague*, and a series of discussions, led by specialists from English, history, French, theology, microbiology, theater, and medicine, demonstrated again the versatility of Camus's book.

Widely taught, the novel nevertheless remains one of those rare texts that stays in print not merely because of academic patronage. Its initial popularity presaged a profusion of horror movies—*The Beast from 20,000 Fathoms* (1953), *Them* (1954), *It Came from beneath the Sea* (1955), *Godzilla* (1956), *Rodan* (1957), and *Mothra* (1959) among them—that offer the specter of monsters menacing the very civilization that has somehow spawned them. Like them, *The Plague* is a post-Hiroshima nightmare, an expression of acute anxiety over a technological sophistication run amuck, in which lethal radiation and grotesque mutations make a mockery of human pretensions of control. Within a strictly literary tradition, Camus is heir to Dostoyevski, Conrad, and Kafka, prophets of the chthonic underside of modern civilization. *The Plague* endures as a sobering reminder that the same collective genius that put a man on the moon also put men and women in Auschwitz and the gulag.

Before the scourge of AIDS made Camus's account of a lethal epidemic seem even more compelling, the general tendency to take the medical dimensions of *The Plague* for granted confirms its own insights into the human capacity for slothful self-deception. If, as Camus himself argued, *The Plague* is more than a chronicle of the Resistance, though it is nothing less than that, it is also more than a prophecy of AIDS, but certainly it is nothing less than *that*. Long after AIDS becomes as distant a memory as the Black Death and the Hundred Years War, *The Plague* will still command attention for its masterfully rendered lesson in humility, its eloquent honesty about a universe that frustrates human understanding and design.

The Plague is the longest and most ambitious book of prose fiction that Camus lived to complete. Its earnest allegorical calculus sometimes seems a bit contrived. And it does not impress through verbal bounty or the plenitude of characters it offers for our acquaintance. *The Plague* is, in comparison with *Moby-Dick* (1851)—the Melville work that Camus read carefully and reverently while writing his own book—a small novel, one deliberately restrained in style and plot. Yet it succeeds in making a virtue of austerity, and an issue of necessity and of the constraints on human action in an inhospitable universe.

What distinguishes *The Plague* from other Camus works is its author's success in portraying his characters not merely as alienated individuals but as social creatures as well, in a society whose codes and compulsions are as absurd as those of the cosmos as a whole. Its prose is scrupulous; its characters are few but unforgettable. In structure and narrative design, *The Plague* offers an ingenious solution to an aesthetic problem that is also an ethical one: How does an artist give cogent form to the painful muddle of human experience?

Of the four contemporary French books that in 1960 Gaëtan Picon assessed as the greatest, *The Plague* seems to have endured best: "If I were asked which French novels published since 1940 are worthy of being called masterpieces, I would answer without hesitation that I see just four: Malraux's *The Walnut Trees of Altenburg*, Bernanos's *Monsieur Ouine*, Sartre's *The Reprieve*, and Camus's *The Plague*."[3] *The Plague* seems the only one that, decades later, an ardent and amateur seeker of truth might still carry about for personal enlightenment and pleasure. "*La Peste* is," declared Germaine Brée, one of the most ardent and prolific of Camus's champions, "within its limits, a great novel, the most disturbing, most moving novel yet to have come out of the chaos of the mid-century."[4] Those limits might be too great to admit of such hyperbole. But by the end of the century, *The Plague* has not lost its capacity to move and disturb.

3

Critical Reception

Within a few weeks of its publication, on 10 June 1947, *La Peste* had already sold 100,000 copies, and its author was transformed into a Left Bank celebrity. Despite the vicissitudes of Camus's reputation, his novel has continued year after year to sell prodigiously. Though French publishers are coy about revealing statistics, it has been estimated that, by 1980, *The Plague* had, in all its myriad editions and translations, sold 3,700,000 copies (corresponding figures for *The Stranger* [1942] are 4,300,000; for *The Fall* [1956] 1,300,000; and for *Exile and the Kingdom* [1957] 930,000).[1] *The Plague* was included in the definitive Pléiade edition of Camus's collected works that, published a mere two years after his death, in effect canonized him by presenting his writings with the same solicitude and in the same prestigious format as those of Racine, Flaubert, and Proust.

The *France-Observateur* reviewer Roger Stéphane joined many other initial reviewers in praising Camus's novel for "the most faithful depiction of daily life under the Occupation."[2] Jean-Paul Sartre, the most influential critic in Paris, perhaps in Europe, saluted the new novel with a footnote on the final page of his study *What Is Literature?*: "Camus' *The Plague*, which has just been published, seems to me a good example of a unifying movement which bases a plurality of critical and constructive themes on the organic unity of a single myth."[3] Though each, and particularly Camus, would express discomfort about the term existentialism, Sartre and Camus were widely regarded as the twin leaders of the existentialist movement, and a new book by either was a major public event. The two would later, after the publication of *The Rebel* in 1951, exchange sharply hostile words and break in one of the most infamous intellectual feuds of the time. Yet the eulogy that Sartre published three days after the shocking death in 1960, of his erstwhile comrade and adversary might also stand as an assessment of *The Plague*: "Camus could never cease to be one of the principal forces in our cultural domain, nor to represent, in his own way, the history of France and of this century."[4]

The book, which was honored with that year's Prix des Critiques, has remained one of the most commercially successful works ever published in France. It is true that some French critics were troubled by certain details, and many continue to be. Writing in Sartre's magazine *Les Temps modernes*, Jean Pouillon, for example, raised questions about the appropriateness of the disease-Occupation analogy, questions that have remained central concerns to critics of the novel. Pouillon faulted *The Plague* for idealizing the Resistance and for creating an artificial framework that pits "a virtuous and oppressed minority against an anonymous and depersonalized aggressor."[5] Both Pouillon and Jean Catesson, reviewing *La Peste* for *Cahiers du sud*,[6] questioned the appropriateness of making the sufferings of the war seem, through the agency of a natural epidemic, unavoidable and inexplicable when, in fact, the Nazis were identifiable human beings who acted out of choice. René Etiemble voiced the disappointment of leftists sympathetic to Moscow when he faulted Camus for abandoning them. He seized on *La Peste* as evidence that the former Resistance editor had aligned himself with the wrong side in the cold war and sarcastically remarked that in the next confrontation with tyranny Rieux would be unable to take his purifying swim in the Mediterranean because the Americans would have polluted it with radioactive material.[7]

The fate of *The Plague* abroad, and especially in North America— where readers are notoriously resistant to anything foreign, particularly in translation—was probably even more remarkable than it was in Europe. Justin O'Brien, who would himself later translate a few of Camus's other books, typified the American reception when, writing for the *New Republic*, he greeted the arrival of *The Plague* with unalloyed enthusiasm: "In French or in English this is a first-rate novel. A sober, tautly written account of a raging bubonic plague in the North African city of Oran, it creates a situation of soul-revealing crisis, and peoples that situation with very real and well differentiated characters. . . . In telling their story of brave resistance, Albert Camus has accomplished a perfect achievement which, despite the unrelieved grimness of the theme, contains great variety, gay humor and stimulating philosophy."[8] Writing in England, for the *Spectator*, Robert Kee was a bit more understated but no less impressed by Camus's achievement: "*The Plague* is a great deal more than the mere statement of a thesis. It is one of those very rare combinations, an intellectual book that is also a good novel."[9]

La Peste has been translated into at least 16 languages, but Camus's popularity has fluctuated in Europe. When he was awarded the Nobel Prize for Literature in 1957, Camus was, after Kipling, the second youngest author ever to receive the high honor. He was also roundly vilified by critics at both ends of the political spectrum for being too young and less deserving than other candidates. Many murmured that, at only three novels and a handful of plays and short stories, his output was simply too sparse to merit the supreme literary accolade. "One wonders," quipped Roger Stéphane in *France-Observateur*, "whether Camus is not on the decline and if, thinking they were honoring a young writer, the Swedish Academy was not consecrating a precocious sclerosis."[10] The Swedish Academy's citation—"for his important literary production, which with clear-sighted earnestness illuminated the problems of the human conscience in our times"—lauded him with a bloated rhetoric that nevertheless recognizes the stylistic lucidity and ethical ambition that have given *The Plague* and other Camus texts wider appeal and greater endurance than works by most other Nobel laureates.

On this side of the Atlantic Camus was regarded with the kind of affection not often felt for mere intellectuals. One of the most respected and influential of American critics, Susan Sontag, expressed the widespread shock and grief over the premature silencing of Camus's voice: "Kafka arouses pity and terror, Joyce admiration, Proust and Gide respect, but no modern writer that I can think of, except Camus, has aroused love. His death in 1960 was felt as a personal loss by the whole literate world."[11] Nevertheless, a sharp reaction in France against what was thought an inflated reputation set in immediately after the automobile accident that killed Camus in 1960. For the next few years, while French fiction was turning toward aesthetics and linguistics and away from politics, Camus's committed stance was out of fashion. In the late 1960s, particularly following the Paris student rebellion of 1968, when political engagement again became a prerequisite for literary homage, Camus, who had opposed ideology and failed in his pathetic attempt to mediate the Algerian war, was marginalized by many as feckless and reactionary. He was denounced as "a bleating boy scout" by one young insurgent, J.-J. Brochier, and was dismissed by most as banal and passé.[12] Armed struggle against the iniquities of imperialist capitalism was in vogue, and Camus, who feared tyranny from the left as much as from the right, was not. His anticommunism was scorned as reactionary and naive. "What Camus is arguing against in *La Peste*," wrote Philip Thody in 1961, as Camus's reputation was declining, "is the myth of violent revolution prevalent in post-war France, a myth with which he himself had briefly sympathised, but which he was to attack in much more detail in *L'Homme révolté*."[13] *The Plague* seemed out of sync in a revolutionary time.

However, in Eastern Europe, which hoarded him and Alexander Solzhenitsyn in clandestine editions, Camus was revered as a foe of totalitarian thought.[14] A decade later, when the horrors of Stalinist gulags were being exposed in the West, he was restored to favor as a prophet of moderation. Camus's consistent contempt for torture and execution became central principles of Amnesty International, the increasingly popular international human rights organization that was awarded the Nobel Prize for Peace in 1977. "Justice cannot be reconciled with violence," wrote Camus in his notes for *The Plague*, and that sentiment has proven more durable than the ideological zealotry of some of his contemporary critics.[15] A group of intellectuals called "the new philosophers," who arose in opposition to the doctrines of 1960s revolutionaries, hailed Camus as a precursor who spoke out forcefully against the dangers of concentrating power in the state and who recognized that left-wing utopias are often a pretext for violence. "He proved quite simply that it was possible to resist, that courage and lucidity were possible," a 1978 book reminded its readers.[16] Later, *The Plague*, whose narrator and other major characters are obsessed with clarity and veracity, could be seen as anticipating poststructuralist and deconstructionist skepticism toward language. "The lexicons that are proposed to us don't fit," wrote Camus, wary of the treachery of words, in 1944. "This is why the most significant works of the 1940's are perhaps not the ones people think, but those that call language and expression once more into question."[17] Camus named texts by Jean Paulhan, Francis Ponge, and Brice Parain as the most significant works of the 1940s, but *The Plague*, which calls language, expression, and much else into question, surely deserves a place on that roster as well. Through all the fluctuations in Camus's reputation, *The Stranger*, *The Plague*, and *The Fall* have never fallen out of print.

In the United States, Camus has always been one of the very few foreign-language novelists—Hermann Hesse is another—who are read widely and voraciously, even, and especially, by nonacademics. His books have been assimilated into American culture as if they were not translations. "Camus," noted Serge Doubrovsky, "is the great writer American literature has waited for and who never came."[18] Sales of the Random House editions of *The Plague* have continued to be abundant and steady—an average of 33,000 copies a year since 1948. [19] Conceded Susan Sontag, "Neither art nor thought of the highest quality is to be found in Camus." She found other compensations, however, in reading Camus: "What accounts for the extraordinary appeal of his work is beauty of another order, moral beauty, a quality unsought by most twentieth-century writers."[20]

American politicians are not noted for their literary interests, yet in a memoir of his friend Robert Kennedy, the journalist Jack Newfield recalled that the senator, who quoted from them frequently, always traveled with a copy of Camus's writings: "He discovered Camus when he was thirty-eight, in the months of solitude and grief after his brother's death. By 1968 he had read, and re-read, all of Camus's essays, dramas and novels. But he more than just read Camus. He memorized him, meditated about him, quoted him and was changed by him."[21] Other activists of the 1960s were similarly affected. In an interview with Robert Penn Warren, Robert Parris Moses, a leader in the Student Nonviolent Coordinating Committee's campaign for civil rights in the South, paid tribute to the moral authority of Albert Camus: "When I was in jail this last time I read through *The Rebel* and *The Plague* again. The main essence of what he says is what I feel real close to—closest to. . . . It's the importance to struggle, importance to recognize in the struggle certain humanitarian values, and to recognize that you have to struggle for people, in that sense, and at the same time, if it's possible, you try to eke out some corner of love or some glimpse of happiness within. And that's what I think more than anything else conquers the bitterness, let's say."[22]

Russians are more familiar with Jack London than Herman Melville, and French readers favor the poetry of Edgar Allan Poe over that of Emily Dickinson. Among American readers, Camus is more widely known and admired than French novelists of greater scope and accomplishment. Camus acknowledged his debt to Ernest Hemingway—who, in turn, learned much from Gustave Flaubert—and some of his appeal on this side of the Atlantic may be due to the "Americanness" of his style. Some of it must also stem, however, from his work's being much less dependent than Stendhal's or Proust's on the particular intricacies of French or France. He translates well because he developed a style dedicated to the classical values of restraint, frugality, and lucidity, and because, as an outsider himself in France, he was intent on capturing universal truths. The American novelist William Styron was exhilarated by Camus's tonic recognition of a bleak cosmos: "Camus was a great cleanser of my intellect, ridding me of countless sluggish ideas and, through some of the most unsettling pessimism I had ever encountered, causing me to be aroused anew by life's enigmatic promise."[23] The South African playwright Athol Fugard also found a kindred spirit in the Camus who was passionate about social and cosmic justice but wary of its attainment. "I would be happy to spend the next ten years deepening my understanding and appreciation of this man—and rereading and again rereading everything he has written," wrote Fugard in 1963. "Camus sounds out and charts the very oceans of experience, feeling and thought, on which I find myself sailing at this moment. His importance to me is monumental. Reading Camus is like finding, and for the first time, a man speaking my own language."[24]

Personal testimonials to the power of *The Plague* continued through the 1980s, though it no longer seemed quite as necessary to argue for the novel's place in the modern canon. Curiously, the quantity of recent scholarly writing on *The Plague* has been sparse relative to the enormous readership it has enjoyed within the academy and beyond. The book does not provide the same hermeneutical challenge as do more deliberately, cleverly hermetic texts. Each of Camus's other two novels has received more attention in print than has *The Plague*, and so, too, have some less widely read novels—Alain Robbe-Grillet's *The Erasers* (1953) for example. By its fourth decade, the novel had attained the ultimate triumph and horror of a conscientious author: being taken for granted.

The Plague is discussed in passing in the proliferating general studies of Camus's literary career, and it is accorded an important place within each of the two full-scale biographies of Camus that were published within three years of each other, 1979 and 1982, by Herbert R. Lottman and Patrick McCarthy, respectively. Individual studies have applied most of the newly fashionable theories and methodologies to analysis of *The Plague*. It has been subjected to the scrutinies of narratologists, semioticians, feminists, and anti-imperialists. The novel has been metafictionalized (Fitch, Kellman), neopsychoanalyzed (Gassin), and deconstructed (Barnett). It has been examined as an exercise in reader response (Zimmerman) and for its strategy of gender construction (Rizzuto). It has received considerable attention as a glimpse at the other, as a product of a non-European culture (Amoia, Grenier 1987, Lenzini, Roy). It is likely to endure much more.

A Reading

Death as an Enemy (The First Outbreak of Cholera at a Masked Ball in Paris, 1831), 1851,
Gustav Richard Steinbrecher (German, 1828–1887)
Phildelphia Museum of Art: SmithKline Corporation Collection

4

The Mysterious Narrator

This progress you will see easily in that old English ballad "Turpin Hero" which begins in the first person and ends in the third person. The dramatic form is reached when the vitality which has flowed and eddied round each person fills every person with such vital force that he or she assumes a proper and intangible esthetic life. The personality of the artist, at first a cry or a cadence or a mood and then a fluid and lambent narrative finally refines itself out of existence, impersonalises itself, so to speak.
    —James Joyce, *A Portrait of the Artist as a Young Man*[1]

Organized into five sections, *The Plague* recounts the collective ordeal of Oran, Algeria, from 16 April "194_" until the following February. Part 1 introduces us to Oran, notes the sudden proliferation of dead rats and sick humans, and outlines how reluctant officials eventually decide to declare an epidemic. Part 2, whose tone is set by Father Paneloux's somber first sermon, details how each of the principal characters—Rieux, Tarrou, Grand, Rambert, Paneloux, Othon, and Cottard—copes with the plague. Part 3 is a brief discursive interlude in the story in which the narrator offers general observations about life under the quarantine, paying particular attention to the plight of parted lovers. Part 4 offers Paneloux's very different sermon, a change of heart for Rambert, the death of the magistrate Othon's son, and increased attention to Tarrou as a fighter of plague. In part 5, Tarrou dies, the plague subsides, Cottard is arrested, and the narrator reveals himself. The five sections with which Camus organizes his novel echo the traditional structure of a five-act neoclassical French tragedy.

"The unusual events described in this chronicle occurred in 194_ at Oran," the narrator begins. "Everyone agreed that, considering their somewhat extraordinary character, they were out of place there. For its ordinariness is what strikes one first about the town of Oran, which is merely a large French port on the Algerian coast, headquarters of the Prefect of a French Department" (3). What might strike readers of Fyodor Dostoyevski is how much the first paragraph of Camus's *The Plague* resembles the opening of *The Possessed* (aka *The Devils*), the 1871 Russian novel that Camus was to adapt into a three-act play in 1959: "Before discussing the extraordinary events which took place so recently in our town, hitherto not remarkable for anything in particular, I find it necessary, since I am not a skilled writer, to go back a little and begin with certain biographical details concerning our talented and greatly esteemed Stepan Trofimovich Verkhovensky. I hope these details will serve as an introduction to the social and political chronicle of our town, while the story I have in mind will come later."[2]

Both novels emphasize the drabness of the setting as a foil to the exceptional experiences about to be related. Both Dostoyevski and Camus begin their stories in the voice of an unnamed, self-effacing narrator who presents himself as the spokesman for the town. And both insist on the word *chronicle* to characterize the account they proceed to provide.

Camus begins his book with an epigraph from the preface to volume 3 of *Robinson Crusoe* (1719), a novel whose author, Daniel Defoe, was also well known to Camus for having written *A Journal of the Plague Year* (1722), a fictional account of life in London during a seventeenth-century epidemic. Camus situates his own fiction within a tradition of plague narratives that also includes the Book of Job, Thucydides' *History of the Peloponnesian War*, Boccaccio's *Decameron* (1353), Thomas Dekker's *The Wonderful Year* (1603), the Pied Piper legend, Edgar Allan Poe's "King Pest" (1835) and "The Masque of the Red Death" (1842) Alessandro Manzoni's *The Betrothed* (1825–42), Jean Giono's *The Horseman on the Roof* (1952), Thomas Mann's *Death in Venice* (1912), Gabriel Garcìa Màrquez's *Love in the Time of Cholera* (1988), and J. M. Coetzee's *Waiting for the Barbarians* (1980). Released in 1950, three years after Camus's novel,

The Mysterious Narrator

Elia Kazan's film *Panic in the Streets* stars Richard Widmark as a health officer in pursuit of Jack Palance, who is suspected of both murder and spreading pneumonic plague. In 1957 the Swedish director Ingmar Bergman used the Black Death in fourteenth-century northern Europe as the context for a metaphysical drama in *The Seventh Seal*. Horton Foote's *1918*, starring Matthew Broderick, William Converse-Roberts, and Hallie Foote, portrays the effects of the influenza epidemic on a small Texas town. For nonfictional background to the history of plagues, one could—and Camus did—consult the 1897 book *La Défense de l'Europe contre la peste* (Europe's Defense against the Plague), which happens to have been written by Adrien Proust, the physician father of a modern novelist Camus much admired, Marcel Proust.

What distinguishes Camus's book from other plague stories, however, is the fact that it is a mystery novel, and what makes it an unusual mystery novel is the fact that it is not a whodunit; we know from the start—even before the cautious authorities are willing to acknowledge an epidemic—that it is not the butler but the plague that is killing off the people of Oran. Instead, it is a "whotoldit": Who is narrating *The Plague*? And why does he camouflage himself until the final eight pages of the book?

We begin with a rather impersonal overview of a rather impersonal town. There is, according to our unidentified guide, nothing to identify Oran in a lineup of dozens of other drab seaboard settlements—"For its ordinariness is what strikes one first about the town of Oran, which is merely a large French port on the Algerian coast, headquarters of the Prefect of a French Department." The first section of the novel confines itself to a general description of banal appearances and customs within the nondescript town of Oran. Oranians are referred to as "our townsfolk," not by proper names, even after separate characters are finally introduced. No individual intrudes until page 7, and no stylistic idiosyncrasies obtrude from sentences that pretend they could have been written by anyone. Instead of personal pronouns, we find the French word *on*, which is literally—and stiffly—translated as "one" but which Stuart Gilbert most often renders into English as a vague "we." "We must not exaggerate" (5), insists someone anxious not to stand out, and the very use of "we" keeps him or her from protruding. The French text also makes abundant use of reflexive and passive constructions; instead of telling us that a particular person performs an action, the narrator elusively announces that something is done.

The Plague is a tale that would have us believe that no one in particular wrote it, that it is in fact telling itself. It is repeatedly referred to as a "chronicle," and what defines a chronicle is that chronology, not individual imagination, determines the order of events. Veracity, not invention, is the virtue of a chronicle, and an author's byline would be a disturbing reminder of the possibility of eccentricity and fabrication. Scrupulous about establishing that this is no private fantasy, the anonymous narrator defines, through a detached third-person pronoun, the role of the chronicler: "His business is only to say: 'This is what happened,' when he knows that it actually did happen, that it closely affected the life of a whole populace, and that there are thousands of eyewitnesses who can appraise in their hearts the truth of what he writes" (6). To reinforce his credibility as "chronicler" or "historian," the narrator explains that the narrative will be relying on three kinds of evidence: his own direct observations, the accounts of other eyewitnesses, and reliable documents that he has acquired.

Of course, we cannot ignore the fact that, whoever it is, there is a narrator, one who (in a parenthetical reference to the fact that his "identity will be made known in due course" [6]) teases us with the promise of future revelation. We mentally muster the unusual suspects. Is it Tarrou? Rambert? Rieux? Grand? Madame Rieux? Cottard? Paneloux? The insistence that Dr. Bernard Rieux's initial reaction of uncertainty and surprise to the advent of plague "was the same as that of the great majority of our townsfolk" (34) might cause the reader to begin to develop suspicions. Later, the narrator will contend that discussing the trauma of exile is not a private catharsis, "that he can set down here, as holding good for all, the feeling he personally had and to which many of his friends confessed" (65). Specifically, we are told about the plight of parted lovers, "who present the greatest interest and of whom the narrator is, perhaps, better qualified to speak" (68). To whom do they present the greatest interest if not to one of those lovers himself, who doth protest too much by reiterating that the attitudes and emotions expressed belong to everyone in town? Many Oranians are not parted lovers, and it is possible they would consider the emphasis on parted lovers a distortion of the collective experience. Yet the chronicle of Oran is presented in terms of the theme of enforced separation. Camus had at an early stage, in fact, used *"Les Exilés"* (The Exiles) as a working title for what was to become *The Plague*, his novel of separation.

Bernard Rieux has, of course, parted from his wife just before the onset of the plague, when she leaves Oran for a sanatorium in the mountains. Because of the quarantine, she cannot return, and she dies before it is possible to join her husband again. By page 271 it probably surprises few readers when Rieux at last steps forward and admits to being the narrator, though again proclaiming that he has been "an honest witness" (272) who has merely reported what everyone experienced. Still reluctant to abandon the mask of the third-person "he," Rieux says of himself: "Whenever tempted to add his personal note to the myriad voices of the plague-stricken, he was deterred by the thought that not one of his sufferings but was common to all the others and that in a world where sorrow is so often lonely, this was an advantage" (272). What was the advantage of concealment, of suppressing the "I" with a "he"?

The reader is much less inclined than Rieux himself to question his appropriateness as storyteller. As a dedicated physician, he occupies a uniquely central position in the efforts of Oran to contend with the plague. Rieux's medical responsibilities bring him into contact with a wide range of characters, and he is professionally analytic and articulate. Furthermore, the role of doctor is a crucial one for the novel's allegory. The vital struggle against the plague is most obviously carried on by someone occupationally dedicated to healing, though it remains moot what a doctor, or anyone, can possibly accomplish against a force as implacable as the deadly disease that abruptly arrives in Oran and, oblivious to Dr. Castel's serum, departs on its own terms. In a 1948 interview in which he confessed greater affinity with Rieux than with the secular saint Tarrou, Camus described the role of the writer in terms reminiscent of his fictional Oran doctor, who is, of course, also a writer: "Writers are on the side of life, against death and suffering. It is the only justification for their strange calling."[3] Rieux persists in his strange Hippocratic calling even when his labors seem wholly gratuitous, when the epidemic seems to claim its victims at random and in defiance of medical measures. Even the effectiveness of the antitoxin that is ultimately developed to defeat the bacillus, however temporarily, remains ambiguous. These developments in the plot are clearly important to the articulation of the novel's themes, to its ethical questions about how to behave in a time of plague. But the more tantalizing question remains: Why does Camus adopt the narrative strategy he does?

Agatha Christie provided a clever twist to the whodunit *The Murder of Roger Ackroyd* (1926) by concluding it with the revelation that, rather than any of the other characters we suspect along the way, the culprit is in fact the narrator, the man who—much more dispassionately than King Oedipus in his quest to discover the murderer of his predecessor-father Laius—has all along been amassing clues that point to himself. A similar technique may be found in the tales of Poe. We ordinarily confer trust on someone who seems to be taking us into his confidence enough to serve as our narrator. But in such works as "The Cask of Amontillado" (1846) or "The Tell-Tale Heart" (1843), progressive revelations only assure us that our initial faith was misplaced and that we have accepted the authority of a lethal psychopath. *The Plague* shares with such narratives a certain shock of revelation, of the belated disclosure of the author's identity. Rieux's "chronicle," however, startles less through the discovery that the narrative norm has been established by a patently abnormal figure than through the realization that there is a narrator at all. It is not, as he tries to pretend, a vaguely communal voice lacking the messy particularities of personality. We do learn some distinctive details about Rieux's age and appearance, but only when Rieux reproduces Tarrou's diary notes, not because he himself volunteers any individuating information: "Looks about thirty-five. Moderate height. Broad shoulders. Almost rectangular face. Dark, steady eyes, but prominent jaws. A biggish, well-modeled nose. Black hair, cropped very close. A curving mouth with thick, usually tight-set lips. With his tanned skin, the black down on his hands and arms, the dark but becoming suits he always wears, he reminds one of a Sicilian peasant" (27). Even with Tarrou's description, Rieux is probably not a figure who would stand out in a crowd.

Rieux struggles unsuccessfully to deny the subjectivity lurking behind his objective pose. His efforts raise an issue that emerged in American nonfiction of the 1960s when a movement called "new journalism" was proclaiming the speciousness of a reporter's neutrality. About two-thirds of the way through *Friendly Fire* (1976), a professionally detached account of an Iowa family's anguish over a son, Michael Mullen, reported killed in Vietnam "by artillery fire from friendly forces," the author, C. D. B. Bryan, announces that he can no longer continue with the pretense of having no attitude of his own toward the drama. The remainder is narrated in first-person, with the author as much a character as anyone else in the story.

The final scene of *The Plague* explains much about the novel's narrative strategy. The epidemic has been officially declared defeated, and for the first time in many, many months, the gates of Oran are swung open. With the lifting of the quarantine, couples are reunited after an agonizingly long separation, and the crowded streets resound with public jubilation. Yet one man is isolated and forlorn despite the physical proximity of thousands of celebrants—"on his way to the outskirts of the town, [Rieux] walked alone in an uproar of bells, guns, bands, and deafening shouts" (268). Throughout the long, grim struggle against the plague, one of Rieux's few consolations has been his dream of the day when his wife would rejoin him and their marriage would make a new start. Just as Oran is returning to normal, however, Rieux receives a telegram from the sanatorium informing him that his wife is dead. Rieux's preoccupation with the themes of exile and separation and, in fact, his decision to add the role of narrator to that of physician are clarified by the final, poignant image of a bereaved widower futilely trying to lose himself in the rejoicing mob.

This same tension between individual and society is apparent in Camus's short story "The Artist at Work," published in French as "Jonas" in his 1957 collection *L'Exil et le royaume*. Jonas Gilbert, a painter obsessed with his art, is torn between a lonely dedication to his work and the tow of family and friends. The story concludes with Jonas's breakdown. A friend, Rateau, climbs up to Jonas's secluded studio and examines his latest project, a "canvas, completely blank, in the center of which Jonas had merely written in very small letters a word that could be made out, but without any certainty as to whether it should be read *solitary* or *solidary*."⁴ Rieux can be understood as a *solitary* aspiring to be *solidary*. It is a movement embodied not only in the structure of *The Plague* but in the shape of Camus's career as well.

Of the three novels published during Camus's lifetime, his first, *The Stranger*, portrays an alienated man, Meursault, condemned to irreparable estrangement. With a larger cast of characters, *The Plague* portrays isolate individuals struggling for a common objective and identity. Camus's last published novel, *The Fall*, is the bizarre monologue of a grotesque misanthrope who nevertheless, employing the pronoun "you" throughout, aims to implicate his listener (and reader) in a personal story that he hopes will stand as a microcosm of modern Western history. In a 1955 letter to the French critic Roland Barthes, Camus himself noted that his development from *The Stranger* to *The Plague* had been in terms of a movement from *solitaire* to *solidaire*: "Compared to *The Stranger*, *The Plague* does, beyond any possible discussion, represent the transition from an attitude of solitary revolt to the recognition of a community whose struggles must be shared. If there is an evolution from *The Stranger* to *The Plague*, it is in the direction of solidarity and participation."⁵ *The Rebel*, a philosophical meditation published four years after *The Plague*, also marks that transition. "In absurdist experience," it argues, "suffering is individual. But from the moment when a movement of rebellion begins, suffering is seen as a collective experience. Therefore the first progressive step for a mind overwhelmed by the strangeness of things is to realize that this feeling of strangeness is shared with all men and that human reality, in its entirety, suffers from the distance which separates it from the rest of the universe. The malady experienced by a single man becomes a mass plague."⁶ The statement reads like an account of Camus's evolution from the depiction of individual suffering in *The Stranger* to the communal malady of *The Plague*.

That same process occurs within *The Plague* itself, not only in how Rieux—and Rambert, Paneloux, and Grand—develop as social beings during the plague. But Rieux's movement from lonely widower to chronicler and back to lonely widower within each separate reading of the novel reenacts the metamorphosis from *solitaire* to *solidaire* so important to Camus. Of course, Rieux's position as physician, as administrator of Oran's sanitary squads, sets him apart from the rest of his fellow citizens, but being a doctor during an epidemic also means trying to reintegrate himself into the common populace. And like Rieux, Camus aspired to be a voice for more than his own private concerns. "*The Plague*," Camus wrote in his notebook in 1946, "ought to be the first attempt at shaping a collective passion."[7]

By the time of his Nobel Prize speech in Stockholm on 10 December 1957, Camus was describing his own role as writer in terms of an arc of separation and reconciliation similar to that of Rieux's:

> Art is not, to my mind, a solitary pleasure. It is a means of moving the greatest number of men by offering them a privileged image of common suffering and joy. It thus requires the artist not to isolate himself; it submits him to the most humble and most universal truth. And the one who has chosen the calling of artist precisely because he felt different learns rather quickly that he cannot nourish his art or his difference except by acknowledging his kinship with all. The artist creates himself in this perpetual round-trip between himself and others, midway between the beauty that he cannot do without and the community from which he cannot wrench himself.[8]

Camus—the pied-noir awkwardly afoot in Paris who was forever making common cause against oppression, though wary of movements, groups, and institutions—might have been speaking about Rieux as much as himself.

In the manner of the *ouroboros*, the mythological icon of a snake swallowing its own tail, the end of *The Plague* thus leads back to its beginning. Rieux's "I" has been separated from the collective "we" in which he has submerged himself for most of the story. Excruciatingly solitary during the city's supreme moment of solidarity, Rieux vows to reunite himself with the living and dead of Oran by becoming the

city's chronicler. By losing himself in the role of impersonal spokesman, Rieux will try to overcome the separations of selfhood and to
will himself into unity with his fellow townsfolk, reversing the slippage
from "he" to "I" that occurred for him with the lifting of the quarantine. To follow the doctor's efforts to accomplish that, we must turn
back to the opening sentence of his chronicle.

5

Sisyphus in Oran

Writing a book is a horrible, exhausting struggle, like a long bout of some painful illness.

—George Orwell, "Why I Write"[1]

Each subsequent reading of *The Plague* thus propels the reader back to start again. Dr. Bernard Rieux's decision to take on the task of "being the chronicler of the troubled, rebellious hearts of our towns-people under the impact of the plague" (121) is best understood by returning to that task, the story we have just finished reading. A self-begetting novel, a narrative that recounts its own origins, *The Plague* also offers no conclusion. Each time the reader and the narrator arrive at the lifting of the quarantine, we are directed back to the opening page, to the chronicle that Rieux will write, which will explain how he came to his decision, which will. . . .

The Plague is one of many modern novels easier reread than read. Its design is suggestively similar to what appealed to Camus about the writings of Franz Kafka: "The whole art of Kafka consists in forcing the reader to reread. His endings—or his absence of endings—suggest explanations which, however, do not appear clearly and require the story to be reread from another point of view to be justified."[2] This circular narrative pattern also recalls the story of Sisyphus, the figure in Greek mythology whom Camus appropriated to embody his vision of an absurd universe. *The Myth of Sisyphus*—which was published in 1942 though it had been finished in 1941, shortly before Camus began writing *The Plague*—became the best known of his philosophical writings and the most accessible of the nonfiction works to emerge out of the popular movement loosely known as existentialism, which conceived of the individual adrift in a contingent, absurd universe. In *The Myth of Sisyphus*, Camus reviews the legend of the Corinthian king who, for refusing to accede to death, was punished by the gods with unremitting torment. For all of eternity, Sisyphus is condemned to push a heavy boulder up a steep mountainside. Each time he is on the verge of attaining the peak, the boulder rolls to the bottom of the mountain and Sisyphus must begin his futile task again. For all his strenuous, repetitive labors, Sisyphus can never hope to accomplish anything, yet he persists in pushing his burden up the slope, and for that reason Camus dubs him "the absurd hero." "His scorn of the gods, his hatred of death, and his passion for life won him that unspeakable penalty in which the whole being is exerted toward accomplishing nothing."[3]

Camus concludes his study of human existence as superfluous, redundant, and unredeemed by transcendence with the assertion of a paradox. Sisyphus is aware of the absurdity of his condition, and yet his very consciousness of it enables him to exult in the futility of a meaningless cycle: "Sisyphus, proletarian of the gods, powerless and rebellious, knows the whole extent of his wretched condition: it is what he thinks of during his descent. The lucidity that was to constitute his torture at the same time crowns his victory. There is no fate that cannot be surmounted by scorn."[4] *The Myth of Sisyphus* ends with its most famous and intriguing sentence: "One must imagine Sisyphus happy."[5]

One must also imagine Rieux—whose name is suggestively similar to *rieur*, one who laughs—happy in his absurd way. He, too, is set a task, as doctor and narrator, that promises no accomplishment or completion, and yet he returns to the struggle, again and again. It is not apparent that, for all his unremitting efforts, Rieux manages to save the life of a single victim of the plague, though day after day he goes back to the sickrooms. And never entirely successful in losing himself as impersonal chronicler, he is forever beginning his story again. The circular design of *The Plague*, without beginning or end, embodies the labors of Sisyphus. As Camus notes in *The Myth of Sisyphus*, "[T]he last pages of a book are already contained in the first pages."[6] Though exasperated by a universe of relentless, pointless suffering and by a plot line that leads nowhere but whence it started, the reader is braced by a new awareness. One must imagine the reader happy.

Appropriate to the world of Sisyphus, the word *recommencer*— to begin again—recurs again and again in the French text of Camus's novel. Though the final words of the book remind us that the plague never dies, that it merely lies dormant, ready to "rouse up its rats again and send them forth to die in a happy city" (278), the characters plan to begin their lives again after the plague. The curious old man whom Tarrou early in the novel observes spitting on cats rejoices in the reappearance of the animals after the disease has vanished, because it means that he can recommence his ritual of expectoration. Rieux looks to resume his marriage after the lifting of the quarantine, just as the municipal clerk Joseph Grand hopes to start all over again with his estranged wife Jeanne. Grand is, of course, also forever recommencing the sentence he is writing until he gets it right, and he is sentenced to begin his life again after almost succumbing to the plague. Because of a ten-month embargo against anything entering the city, the townsfolk are forced to go see the same movies again and again, and the touring opera company that is trapped by the quarantine in Oran performs the same production of Gluck's *Orfeo ed Euridice* every Friday, month after month, to capacity audiences that keep returning to see the curtain rise on act 1 again and again.

One of the few moments of relief that Rieux and Tarrou find from the grim pressures of fighting the plague occurs toward the end of part 4. Uncharacteristically taking advantage of their special privileges, they drive just beyond the boundaries of the quarantine, to the harbor from which Oran has been cut off. The two friends jump into the sea for a resuscitating swim. But as soon as it is over, Rieux insists *"qu'il fallait maintenant recommencer"* (it was now necessary to begin again) (1429)[7]—in Gilbert's translation, "they must set their shoulders to the wheel again" (233).

Like Sisyphus and his boulder, Rieux's eccentric asthma patient spends his days in bed performing a pointless task: the 75-year-old Spaniard methodically transfers dried peas from one pan to another, only to begin again transferring the peas back into the original pan when he has completed each cycle. More dramatically, Raymond Rambert is a portrait in recommencement. A journalist assigned by his Parisian newspaper to investigate sanitary conditions among the Arabs of Oran, Rambert is caught by the quarantine within a city he does not consider home. Desperate to return to the woman he loves in Paris, he enters into elaborate negotiations with underworld smugglers to get himself out of Oran. Clandestine plans are made, but each time he is on the verge of success something goes wrong, and Rambert must start all over again to plot his illegal departure. Ultimately, despite all his scheming, Rambert declines to go through with his escape. He returns to Oran from the city limits, determined to make common cause with its citizens in their fight against the plague. When the quarantine is finally ended, Rambert, like everyone else, is intent on beginning again. In Rieux's final glimpse of him, Rambert is passionately reunited with the woman he has not seen for most of a year, eager to begin their relationship again.

In his 1957 Nobel Prize speech, Camus spoke of his generation as having arisen again out of the ashes of military conflagration. Referring both to the reconstruction of Europe and to his own literary efforts, he declared: "We found it necessary to create an art by which to live through a time of catastrophe, to be born a second time, and struggle onward, eyes open, against the instinct of death at work in our history." In his Sisyphean conception of history, he recognized that "[e]ach generation, no doubt, believes itself dedicated to remaking the world."[8]

Rieux's earliest descriptions of Oran stress the town's devotion to habit and ritual, the fact that "you can get through the days there without trouble, once you have formed habits. And since habits are precisely what our town encourages, all is for the best" (5). Habits are gestures recommenced, and though the plague makes certain habits—like spitting on cats—impossible, it encourages new ones—like attending *Orfeo*. When the plague departs, the people of Oran return to their old routines, recommence their old rituals of recommencement. However, awareness of a habit defamiliarizes it and enables us to transcend it even as we perpetuate the same cycle of activities. We must imagine ourselves happy in our habits, like Sisyphus. Meditating on the experience of the absurd, Camus wrote in his notebook that we "should endure this experience without flinching, with complete lucidity."[9] Rieux's unsentimental awareness of Oran's ordeal represents the kind of curiously cheerful attitude that Camus prescribes for Sisyphus and all the rest of us caught in an absurd universe.

A qualified happiness is, in fact, the final note to Camus's rather grim novel. The plague has dissipated, but as the narrator notes, it remains dormant, ready to begin again at any moment. The book's final image is of how the plague might "rouse up its rats again and send them forth to die in a happy city." Because of the rules of French syntax, in which adjectives often follow nouns, the French text is able to conclude everything with a happy word: "*la peste réveillerait ses rats et les enverrait dans une cité heureuse*" (1474). Or one must imagine it so.

6

Hippocratic Detachment

Rieux's predicament is exacerbated by his elite position as a physician, someone whose profession requires detachment from the ordinary people he is committed to serving. In an unusual moment of personal revelation to Tarrou, Rieux explains that one of the reasons he became a doctor was the personal ambition of social mobility. Going to medical school was one of the few ways to escape from the working class— "I had a desire for it, because it meant a career like another, one that young men often aspire to. Perhaps, too, because it was particularly difficult for a workman's son, like myself" (117). Rieux's is the not uncommon fate of a proletarian whose professional achievement estranges him from his origins. But another way of viewing his actions throughout *The Plague* and his chronicling of the plague is as the ardent attempt of a successful social climber to step back down from his lonely heights.

The Plague makes reference to a local medical association, and Oran evidently has enough doctors to form the health committee that convenes in the Prefect's office in part 1 to consider prophylactic measures against the lethal disease that has recently appeared in town. However, Oran's physicians seem scarcely more of a fraternity among themselves than they are integral parts of the community they treat. Aside from Rieux, only two are mentioned by name—Richard and Castel—and they appear but briefly. For most of his account of the city's ordeal, Rieux is the only doctor around.

Chairman of the medical association, Dr. Richard is reluctant to convene its members and to take any collective action against the epidemic. Despite increasing and irrefutable evidence, he cautions against jumping to hasty conclusions and acting precipitously. Loath to take the initiative in dealing with the disease, he repeatedly insists that fighting the plague is "outside his province" (28). Like Raymond Rambert, Richard refuses to see the plague as his battle. Even when the evidence of a massive public health crisis becomes too blatant to deny, Richard equivocates; but after prodding from Rieux, he concedes: "We are to take the responsibility of acting as though the epidemic were plague" (47).

It is a less than forthright declaration, in striking contrast to the straightforward rhetoric that Rieux insists upon. By creating one physician, Richard, who is irresolute and evasive, Camus highlights the candor and courage of another, Rieux. Much later in the novel, when the daily toll of deaths ceases to rise, Richard calls a meeting of medical leaders to make the buoyant announcement that the plague has begun to ebb. In reality, as the honest doctor who narrates the story informs us, the disease is still at its most virulent stage. And the meeting never takes place, because Richard dies of plague.

In sharp contrast to Richard, a physician who uses his privileged position to hide from the truth, is Castel, the blunt old doctor who, in Rieux's eyes, is a paragon of the Hippocratic calling. It is Castel who, during his long career, has seen plague in China and Paris and who first gets Rieux to admit what is happening in Oran: "Come now, Rieux, you know as well as I do what it is" (33). It is, of course, plague, and at Castel's impetus, Rieux immediately pronounces the word for the first time in the book. At the health committee's meeting in the Prefect's office, Castel brusquely cuts through Richard's euphemisms and circumlocutions to force the other doctors to confront the harsh reality they face.

Like Rieux, Castel has a wife who is separated from him by the quarantine of Oran. Madame Castel happens to be visiting a neighboring town when the gates of Oran are closed. Rieux marvels at the fact that, though the Castels are far from being passionate newlyweds and their marriage is imperfect, Madame Castel chooses to risk her life to return to her husband. Noting that "this ruthless, protracted separation enabled them to realize that they could not live apart" (64), Rieux, separated forever from a wife who dies beyond the closed ramparts of Oran, reflects upon another doctor who is less isolated. To try to overcome his solitude, Rieux throws himself into the struggle against the common menace of the plague bacillus. So, too, does the exemplary figure of Castel, who spends the many arduous months of epidemic trying to develop a serum to defeat an invincible foe. In the pestilential universe of Camus's novel, physicians cannot even heal themselves. Theirs is merely a more vivid case of the futile human match against mortality.

7

Grand and the Aversion to Grandiloquence

Modern fiction, like Alberto Giacometti's emaciated, skeletal sculptures, projects a diminished sense of human possibility. Heroes like Achilles, Aeneas, Beowulf, Roland, and even Indiana Jones—characters whose courage or prowess or wisdom exceeds our own—are absent from the most influential novels of the twentieth century, which are more likely to feature antiheroes, figures who, like Kafka's Gregor Samsa or Hemingway's Jake Barnes, are deficient physically or spiritually or both. It is hard to think of a single character in the Sisyphean universe that Camus creates in *The Plague* who would satisfy the classical definition of hero. Rieux, who notes that the most striking thing about Oran is how unstriking, how ordinary it is, seems uncomfortable with the category of hero. He concedes, however, that for many readers a story needs a hero, and if so, he is willing to nominate one—Joseph Grand: "Yes, if it is a fact that people like to have examples given them, men of the type they call heroic, and if it is absolutely necessary that this narrative should include a 'hero,' the narrator commends to his readers, with, to his thinking, perfect justice, this insignificant and obscure hero who had to his credit only a little goodness of heart and a seemingly absurd ideal" (126).

A meek, middle-aged functionary whose very name, Grand, makes a mockery of his insignificance, he is even, four pages earlier, described as having "nothing of the hero about him" (122). With unfulfilled promises of a promotion, Grand has been employed for 22 years in the meager post of "temporary assistant municipal clerk" (41). It is not surprising that, after years of poverty and monotony with him, Grand's wife Jeanne has left him for someone else. "What chance had any passion of surviving such conditions?" (75), asks Rieux, and through him, Camus, who knew the hardships of poverty and wartime deprivation. Yet Rieux, who has treated the needy Grand gratis for constriction of the aorta, comes to admire the heartfelt dedication this unexceptional bureaucrat brings to the struggle against the plague. He sees him as "the true embodiment of the quiet courage that inspired the sanitary groups. He had said yes without a moment's hesitation and with the large-heartedness that was a second nature with him" (123). It is precisely because Grand lacks the grandeur of classical heroes yet persists in his arduous task that he is a hero to Rieux—and also, presumably, to Camus, who finds more to respect in Sisyphus than in Odysseus.

Rieux does not dwell at any length on what exactly Grand—or anyone else—does to fight the plague. It is not clear that anything they do is especially effective against the implacable foe. But Rieux's chronicle is filled with details of another task to which the clerk is equally dedicated: his book. Grand dreams of writing a novel so exceptional that, after examining the manuscript, the publisher he submits it to will only be able to exclaim: "Hats off!" But that triumphant moment never comes, and is never likely to come. Instead, Grand spends most of Camus's novel obsessively reworking a single sentence. Like Sisyphus, he is forever stepping back from the crowning "Hats off!" goal to start his task anew. Like Camus's monomaniacal painter Gilbert Jonas who, in "The Artist at Work," leaves a blank canvas with a tiny scrawl on it, Grand is a memorable caricature of the modern artist as perfectionist, of actual authors who, like Flaubert and Kafka, were rarely satisfied with their writing and would in fact spend weeks on a single sentence. Grand's kinship with Flaubert, who collected platitudes for his *Dictionnaire des idées reçues* (1881, Dictionary of Accepted Ideas), is underscored by the clerk's "trick of professing to quote some turn of speech from 'his part of the world' (he hailed from Montélimar), and following up with some such hackneyed expression as 'lost in dreams,' or 'pretty as a picture' " (39).

"Evenings, whole weeks, spent on one word, just think!" muses Grand. "Sometimes on a mere conjunction!" (95). "Do not worry," Hemingway told himself when afflicted with writer's block. "You have always written before and you will write now. All you have to do is write one true sentence. Write the truest sentence that you know."[1] But Joseph Grand might well be a projection of some of Camus's own anxieties about literary art, of the apprehensions that kept him laboring half a dozen years on *The Plague* and restricted his total novelistic output to three short books, in addition to the fragment of one, *Le Premier Homme* (The First Man), that he had been working on for a year at the time of his death in 1960. In the journal that he kept while writing *The Plague*, Camus expresses despair that he will ever complete the seemingly interminable project: "In my whole life, never such a feeling of failure. I am not even sure of reaching the end."[2]

Grand is shy about revealing his literary efforts, but Rieux eventually learns that they have consisted of hundreds of variations on a single sentence. In fact, by the time its author succumbs to the plague, Grand has filled 50 pages with different drafts of: "One fine morning in the month of May an elegant young horsewoman might have been seen riding a handsome sorrel mare along the flowery avenues of the Bois de Boulogne" (96). The reader is likely to consider such fanatical devotion to a fundamentally frivolous exercise more than a little absurd and yet respect the author's steadfast refusal to abandon his aesthetic ideals. Though impossible of attainment, those ideals are illustrated by the progress that the sentence undergoes. Like Franz Kafka, who, on his deathbed, demanded that his friend Max Brod burn all his manuscripts, Grand, apparently dying of the plague, insists that Rieux torch his texts. Unlike Brod, Rieux honors the request; but when Grand unexpectedly recovers, he goes back to writing his sentence from scratch. The last version of it that we see, just before the conflagration, reads: "One fine morning in May, a slim young horsewoman might have been seen riding a glossy sorrel mare along the avenues of the Bois, among the flowers" (238–39).

The change is exceedingly, perhaps elusively, subtle, but it is clear from the discussions that Grand has had with Rieux and Tarrou about improving his sentence that he has been moving in the direction of precision and concision. He is striving for *le mot juste*—exactly the right word in the right place, nothing more or less. In Rieux's final reference to Grand, after the plague has ended and the clerk has resumed his literary efforts, though we are not shown the latest version of the sentence, we are left with Grand's last status report: "I've cut out all the adjectives" (276). Suppression of adjectives was the famous lesson that the young Ernest Hemingway took away from Gertrude Stein when he came to her Paris apartment with verbose purple prose. Choose your nouns and verbs carefully enough, and you have no need to add a clumsy modifier. It is a principle of narrative economy honored by many modern writers, including Camus himself, whose terse productions contrast sharply with the big baggy monsters of the nineteenth-century storytellers.

Adjectives—and adverbs—are arguably the most idiosyncratic parts of speech, the words that most reveal the personality of the speaker. By suppressing them, Grand is exemplifying the ideal of self-effacement that is so necessary for solidarity during times of plague and that is so dear to Rieux's own efforts at writing, at being a chronicler rather than a literary artist. Rieux, in fact, associates art with self-expression and self-assertion, both vices that isolate and weaken us in the battle against plague. He repeatedly contends that his role is simply to state, without embellishment, that two plus two equals four. "He has made hardly any changes for artistic effect," Rieux says of himself—"so as not to play false to the facts, and, still more, so as not to play false to himself, the narrator has aimed at objectivity" (163). In writing his chronicle, Rieux is most intent on achieving the impassivity of reportage. He is initially uncooperative with Rambert because he fears that the Parisian newspaper reporter will compromise with candor. "You talk the language of Saint-Just," complains Rambert, to which Rieux replies that "the language he used was that of a man sick and tired of the world he lived in—though he had too much liking for his fellow men—and had resolved, for his part, to have no truck with injustices and compromises with the truth" (11–12).

An aspiring chronicler himself, Rieux is aware of the inadequacy of newspaper writing to represent reality. He notes that, in the earliest stages of the epidemic, the Oran press devotes extensive space to the gruesome spectacle of rats expiring in the streets. When the rats disappear, however, journalism has nothing to say: "For rats died in the street; men in their homes. And newspapers are concerned only with the street" (33). The implication is that newspapers can at best provide only a partial account of the truth—all the more reason for Rieux to mistrust Rambert and to strive to make his own chronicle of Oran under the plague more reliable, because more responsive to the realities of private byways as well as of public thoroughfares.

Like Rambert, Camus, a crusader intent on exposing unpleasant realities of contemporary life, himself served as a reporter on assignment in Oran and other cities. When, in 1939, the censors refused to allow him to publish what he thought was the truth, Camus and his colleague Pia Pascal allowed their newspaper, *Alger-Républicain*, to die rather than print falsehoods or partial truths. Avoiding the melodramatic excess of "creative" writers, Rieux's own text will be "a narrative made with good feelings—that is to say, feelings that are neither demonstrably bad nor overcharged with emotion in the ugly manner of a stage play" (126). The implication seems to be that stage plays are inevitably distortions of the truth.

The only example of a stage play within *The Plague* is a flagrantly melodramatic one, in the root sense of music plus drama. It is the production of Gluck's *Orfeo ed Euridice* that Cottard and Tarrou attend one Friday evening at the Municipal Opera House. Because the touring troupe is trapped in Oran by the quarantine, there is no change in performers or offering, week after week. To Rieux's mind, opera in itself is probably extravagant and frivolous enough. But of all the operas in the repertoire, *Orfeo ed Euridice*, the story of a mortal so endowed with the genius of song that he is able to charm the monsters of Hades and free, at least temporarily, his beloved Eurydice from death, is singularly appropriate to the themes of *The Plague*. Orpheus,

particularly among romantic poets, came to be identified as the arche-
typal artist as hero. The question that thus emerges is: What is the role
and power of the artist during a time of plague? The answer comes in
what actually occurs during the performance that Cottard and Tarrou
happen to attend. In the third act, during his climactic duet with
Eurydice, the singer in the role of Orpheus steps forward to the foot-
lights . . . and drops dead of plague. It is a stunning, and artful, demonstration by the novel of the impotence of art. If even Orpheus is
vulnerable to pestilence, the lesson for Rieux is that the author as
romantic prodigy is at best an Orphic liar. Plain song is the best song
is Camus's cunning refrain.

The colorless, restrained expression to which Grand and Rieux
aspire was a considerable sacrifice for Camus himself. Many of the
early, lyrical essays he collected in *The Wrong Side and the Right Side*
(1937), *Nuptials* (1939), and *Summer* (1954) were in effect prose
poems, often exuberant verbal celebrations of the North African landscape or at least of the vitality of one young, perceptive observer.
The Plague does offer occasional passages of gorgeous prose, as, for
example, when Oran is described as resonant with "one vast rumor
of low voices and incessant footfalls, the drumming of innumerable
soles timed to the eerie whistling of the plague in the sultry air above,
the sound of a huge concourse of people marking time, a never ending,
stifling drone that, gradually swelling, filled the town from end to
end" (168). Passing coveys of starlings and thrushes are described
as frightened off by "the giant flail whirling and shrilling over the
housetops" (169) that is the plague. But Rieux is embarrassed over
eloquence, and Camus's austere style in most of *The Plague* is a deliberate effort to bridle his natural lyricism, as though Van Gogh had
chosen to restrict his palette to brown and gray. "*The Plague* is a
tract," he wrote in his notebooks, perhaps in self-disparagement over
the self-restraint.[3]

If you must use words at all, Rieux seems to be saying, follow
Grand and eschew grandiloquence. Rather than the histrionics of
grand opera, Grand's ideal is more the minimalist style of the telegrams
that are sent and received by those caught within Oran. Commenting
on Father Paneloux's first sermon, Jean Tarrou disparages "rhetoric,"

by which he seems to mean the superfluous multiplication of language that distracts us from veracity: "At the beginning of a pestilence and when it ends there's always a propensity for rhetoric. In the first case, habits have not yet been lost; in the second, they're returning. It is in the thick of a calamity that one gets hardened to the truth—in other words, to silence" (107). If truth is equated with silence, and it seems to be, particularly in the way Rieux's mother is venerated for her mute eloquence, then as soon as Grand, Rieux, Rambert, Tarrou—and Camus—begin to use words, they begin to lie. Any narrator is thus condemned to failure.

8

White Style and Gray Setting

In "Intelligence and the Scaffold," an essay he wrote while working on the first draft of *The Plague*, Camus discusses the ideal of simplicity that inspired the greatest French authors. He admires predecessors like Madame de Lafayette and Stendhal because of the seamlessness of their prose, which seems to have been written with no style at all. But he is careful to note that stylistic transparency is only an illusion, and one that requires a mastery of style to achieve: "People imagine— wrongly—that novels can dispense with style. As a matter of fact, they demand the most difficult style—the kind that does not call attention to itself."[1] A style that does not call attention to itself is precisely what the self-effacing Rieux would hope to achieve in his collective chronicle, or what Grand, in eliminating his adjectives, aims for in his perfect "Hats off!" sentence. It is an ideal that fascinated Camus, torn between *solitaire* and *solidaire*, between individual assertion and self-restraint, throughout his career.

"The great rule of an artist," he contends in that same essay, "is to half forget himself the better to communicate. Inevitably this involves sacrifices." Though the sacrifice is of the self, another half presumably is *not* forgotten. Communion is not the same as total self-extinction, or there would be no one left to do the communing. But Camus insists on the suppression of idiosyncrasy in the artist's creation of a lucid, communicable style: "And this quest for an intelligible language whose role is to disguise the immensity of his objective leads him to say not what he likes but only what he must. A great part of the genius of the French novel lies in the conscious effort to give the order of pure language to the cries of passion."[2]

The notion of self-sacrifice by an author disguising his own distinctive creative processes has obvious applications to Rieux's project as narrator of *The Plague*. The novel is the story of his struggle to develop the pure language of a style that will call attention neither to itself nor to its self-effacing creator. Readers of his chronicle, Rieux hopes, will forget that they are reading a text and lose themselves in the collective experience of Oran, just as the narrator will become lost in the impersonal account. As we have seen, however, Rieux at best only half forgets himself, and the more he insists on objectivity the more his subjectivity obtrudes. "Oh, doctor," exclaims Grand to Rieux, "how I'd like to learn to express myself!" (43). Yet, for each, perfect self-expression would be total self-extinction, a sentence so autonomous that it seems to have written itself, a novel—like *The Plague*—that projects the illusion of self-begetting.

Likewise intrigued by the chimera of a styleless style, of a book so carefully contrived that it has erased all traces of contrivance, Roland Barthes fixed on *The Stranger* as a paradigm of what he called "white writing" (*l'écriture blanche*): "a colourless writing, freed from all bondage to a pre-ordained state of language."[3] Some books flaunt ostentatious verbal devices that make it impossible to ignore the fact that they are, after all, literary artifacts. They exploit the full spectrum of language to embellish the white page with gaudy accounts of colorful personalities. Think of Dickens or Rabelais. But Meursault's story, *The Stranger*, is told with the illusory immediacy that makes us forget the agency of words and the context of storytelling. It is, according to Barthes, the zero degree of writing (*le degré zéro de l'écriture*), "a style of absence that is almost an ideal absence of style."[4] Yet there is surely a paradox in Barthes's cataloging a book whose central actions are a murder and a capital conviction as a prototype of what he calls discursive "innocence." The second half of *The Stranger* is a trial that is in effect a commentary on its first half, and the story as a whole thus doubles back on itself. The self-consciousness of such metacommentary would seem to stain some of the novel's "whiteness."

The concept of neutral, white writing seems even less applicable to *The Plague*, a book that is peopled with writers and orators. Rieux, Tarrou, Grand, Rambert, and Paneloux are all in one way or another wordsmiths, and their conscientious efforts to choose precisely the right phrase in the right place of a chronicle, diary, novel, report, or sermon foregrounds the whole enterprise of writing, calls attention to the fact that *The Plague* is itself a text. It is difficult to forget about the medium of words and lose yourself in the world that those words are pointing to when they also call attention to themselves so persistently. Beginning with its epigraph, from *Robinson Crusoe*, *The Plague* sullies its "innocence" with frequent references to other literary texts; it is as though a movie thriller were forever interrupting the plot and relaxing the suspense with clips from other thrillers. In an analysis of metafictional self-consciousness in *The Plague*, in a chapter titled "The Autoreferential Text," Brian Fitch even counted 170 references to texts within the text of Camus's translucent novel.[5] Though Camus has often been admired more as a prophet than an artist, as an earnest exponent of trendy attitudes, he ought to be read as a conscientious craftsman embarrassed by the inadequacy of his verbal medium. "Love," notes Rieux, reflecting on his relationship to his mother, "is never strong enough to find the words befitting it" (262). And if words fail love, can they be any more successful for other purposes? It is as if all prose is purple prose, never the white writing to which it futilely aspires. *The Plague* is, from its first page to its last, a supremely self-conscious fiction, but what distinguishes it from many of the other metatexts that have metastasized throughout the body of twentieth-century literature is its troubled conscience about its own reflexivity. It longs for a narrative innocence that is sullied by that very longing.

"*Certainement, l'activité romanesque suppose une sorte de refus du réel*" (Novel-writing undoubtedly demands a sort of rejection of reality), wrote Camus in *The Rebel*, three years after suppressing the designation *roman* (novel) from the 1948 reissue of *The Plague*.[6] The narrator of his plague book is obsessed with convincing us that he has neither invented nor embroidered anything. He would not want us to believe that he has created a *novel*, and neither, apparently, would Camus.

A new kind of novel was being imagined in the 1950s by French proponents of what came to be called *le nouveau roman*—the "new novel." As articulated by its leading spokesman, Alain Robbe-Grillet, the new novel would reject the traditional anthropocentrism of fiction, the tendency to insert images and actions into texts because of their human significations. When Honoré de Balzac describes a table in elaborate detail, it is not because of a fascination with the table in itself but rather for what the furniture tells us about its human owner. Robbe-Grillet, instead, called for the restoration of the world of things to their own autonomous unity, not as extensions of human beings. Attacking humanism for the arrogance and bankruptcy of always placing people at the center of a text, he contends that even Camus's absurdist vision is a version of humanism. "Camus does not reject anthropomorphism, he utilizes it with economy and subtlety to give it more weight."[7] Instead of interpreting and thereby deforming the universe for the reader, argues Robbe-Grillet, authors ought to be immersing us in the immediacy of the world as it is in itself.

> But the world is neither significant nor absurd. It *is*, quite simply. That, in any case, is the most remarkable thing about it. And suddenly the obviousness of this strikes us with irresistible force. All at once the whole splendid construction collapses; opening our eyes unexpectedly, we have experienced, once too often, the shock of this stubborn reality we were pretending to have mastered. Around us, defying the noisy pack of our animistic or protective adjectives, things *are there*. Their surfaces are distinct and smooth, *intact*, neither suspiciously brilliant nor transparent. All our literature has not yet succeeded in eroding their smallest corner, in flattening their slightest curve.[8]

Robbe-Grillet recognizes that his program, too, is doomed to failure. It is impossible to use the medium of human words for an unmediated encounter with the nonhuman world.

Despite Robbe-Grillet's condescension toward Camus as an out-moded humanist, the author of *The Plague* anticipated the new novel in his aspiration to reach beyond words and his realization of its impossibility. Jean Tarrou's diary entries come remarkably close to the style and spirit that Robbe-Grillet would become famous for in such novels as *The Voyeur* (1955), *The Erasers* (1953), and *Jealousy* (1957), deliberately enigmatic works that attempt to transcend the distortions of human deliberation. Tarrou's texts are exceptionally spare, and Rieux finds them baffling in their brevity and character of non sequitur. He cannot detect any method to the minute but odd observations that fill his friend's notebooks: *"il s'agit d'une chronique très particulière qui semble obéir à un parti pris d'insignifiance"* (it is a rather peculiar chronicle that seems to be guided by a criterion of *insignificance*) (1236). [9] Rieux is perplexed by the lack of clear purpose to Tarrou's precise but seemingly random descriptions of two bronze lions in front of city hall, the streetcars of Oran, and the snatches of conversations overheard among strangers in what he terms Tarrou's "eccentricities of thought and expression" (25). Of all the passages in Camus's writings, Tarrou's diary entries, in their willingness to present, without imposing a system of signification, a universe of contingent objects, come closest in spirit to *le nouveau roman* of Alain Robbe-Grillet. In its reluctance to indulge in human interpretation, Tarrou's self-effacing prose comes closest to the nonanthropocentric *chosisme* (thingism) that Robbe-Grillet would proclaim a decade after *La Peste*. It also approaches the ideal that Rieux himself suggests for the writer in a time of plague.

CAMUS'S ORAN—AN IMAGE EFFACED

Protagoras's "Man is the measure of all things" became the motto of Renaissance humanists, who displaced medieval theocentrism with an emphasis on human beings here and now. In that sense, as the account of an ordeal unamenable to our understanding or control, *The Plague* is a critique of humanism. Just after the epidemic begins, Rieux describes the surprise of the people of Oran: "In this respect our townsfolk were like everybody else, wrapped up in themselves; in other words they were humanists: they disbelieved in pestilences. A pestilence isn't a thing made to man's measure; therefore we tell ourselves that pestilence is a mere bogy of the mind, a bad dream that will pass away. But it doesn't always pass away and, from one bad dream to another, it is men who pass away, and the humanists first of all, because they haven't taken their precautions" (35). *The Plague* tells the story of the death of anthropocentrism, of the myth of a universe that is attendant and intelligible to the unwise species that arrogantly calls itself *Homo sapiens*. Neither medicine nor theology nor any other human science proves successful in explaining or taming the plague in Oran. And yet, in the manner of a humanist for whom the natural world exists for the convenience and edification of human beings, Camus exploits the plague to make that point. He adopts the strategies of humanism to demonstrate the bankruptcy of humanism.

That paradox is probably clearest in the use of setting throughout *The Plague*. The opening passage insists on workaday Oran as "ordinary," "banal," "bored," "not exceptional," "not particularly exciting." Oran is, we are told in the book's second paragraph, "a thoroughly negative place" (3), devoid of pigeons, trees, and gardens. The landscape is established almost entirely through negation, as though Rieux and Camus wish to use nature as a blank page on which to inscribe their white writing: "Treeless, glamourless, soulless, the town of Oran ends by seeming restful and, after a while, you go complacently to sleep there" (5). The historical Oran, where Camus lived for all of 1941 and most of 1942 with his second wife, Francine Faure, a native of the city, was not nearly as characterless as the narrator of *The Plague*, scrupulous not to exaggerate anything, portrays it. A contemporary local guidebook, probably overstating its charms, describes Oran as an attractive, dynamic, and thriving metropolis: "Everywhere, there are splendid stores, huge banks, administrative and commercial buildings," it declares. "France . . . has made Oran one of the most beautiful cities of France and one of the greatest ports on the Mediterranean where it is good to live. Oran looks toward the future."[10] Camus did not share this buoyant civic pride. In his notebook he dubbed Oran "one of the dustiest cities in the world,"[11] and his 1939 essay "The Minotaur, or, Stopping in Oran" anticipates the landscape of *The Plague* by describing the place as an emotional desert of "extremely ugly buildings"[12] populated by "a nation of shopkeepers."[13] "In the end," contends Camus, "the Oranians are devoured by the Minotaur of boredom."[14]

That Minotaur has also menaced some readers. Reviewing *The Plague* in 1948, Richard McLaughlin anticipated the reactions of some later critics who faulted Camus for the bleakness of his backdrop: "True, the battle against the forces of darkness and ignorance must go on; but it seems to me that the author takes away from the validity and bite of his philosophical argument by shocking us in advance with an unnecessarily gruesome setting."[15] The censors evidently also found his unflattering portrait of Oran unnecessary and denied Camus permission to publish "The Minotaur" in 1939. In a 1953 note to a later edition, he acknowledges the displeasure of Oranians with his comments and, somewhat flippantly, concedes that the city is much more appealing than he allowed: "Violent protests emanating from this beautiful town have in fact assured me that all the imperfections have been (or will be) remedied. The beauties celebrated in this essay have, on the other hand, been jealously protected. Oran, a happy and realistic city, no longer needs writers. It is waiting for tourists."[16]

Oran was unhappy with the image that its most famous writer preserved of it in that essay as well as in *The Plague*. According to Emmanuel Roblès, another Oranian novelist and a friend of Camus's: "The people of Oran don't like *The Plague* very much because, in their opinion, the beginning is not very flattering to their city. Camus showed me (when we were in Paris) some anonymous letters from Oran that criticized him at great length." Roblès notes that, despite the presence of ramparts in *The Plague*, Oran has no municipal gates, that "the city of Oran in the book is a mythical city without any true resemblance to the real Oran."[17] It is one of several ironies that *The Plague*, which is so scrupulously dedicated to the "real" that Camus refused to call it a novel lest it be confused with fantasy, and whose narrator declines any role but that of faithful witness, is so dependent on an artificial setting. But the setting that it contrives is one designed to emphasize neutrality and bareness—in short, the absence of human contrivance.

Intent on creating an unexceptionable Oran of the mind, Camus reduces the city to the image of modern urban anonymity. We are provided with very little sense of the local architecture and none of the distinctiveness of different neighborhoods. Although Rieux says of his fellow citizens that "[t]heir chief interest is in commerce, and their chief aim in life is, as they call it, 'doing business' " (4), we get almost no information about what their businesses are. It seems irrelevant to the purposes of the narrative whether Oran's chief industries are agricultural or manufacturing, whether small shops or large factories are the largest source of employment. *The Plague* attempts nothing like an economic analysis of Oran or of the manner in which the specific organization of production, marketing, and consumption determines the particular set of social relationships that dominate the community. The municipal clerk Joseph Grand, we are told, subsists on a meager income, but no one seems conspicuously wealthy or poor, as though pestilence could overcome economic advantage to level the stratifications of class. Nor does *The Plague* provide much in the way of political analysis, a detailed account of how power is organized and exercised within the city. Early in the story, we learn that the local physicians meet at the office of the Prefect to discuss the rising death rate; but the Prefect remains anonymous, and his authority within the city and in relationship to Algiers and Paris is never explained. The point, perhaps, of such vagueness on the nature and structure of power within the city is that plague effectually renders every human powerless. Attention to the social hierarchy during a time of plague would seem frivolous to Rieux's reductive vision. The Oran in which he lives is a city in which separate individuals—abstracted for the most part from their economic and political functions—attempt to make common cause to fight an implacable foe. The curious absence of telephones reinforces the portrait of an isolated metropolis in which internal contact is difficult and, except for telegrams, external links are virtually severed. The novel contains brief mention of radio, by which something called the Ransdoc Information Bureau provides information on the plague. But that reference seems primarily a pretext for Camus to provide casualty statistics, not to suggest that radio is an important and binding medium in the lives of his characters. There is no sense of an audience attentively listening to broadcasts from either within or without Oran. Rieux's quarantined Oran becomes the archetype of the absurdist universe, a dystopia in which individuals are irreparably solitary, deprived of meaningful action or communication.

The description in "The Minotaur" of Oran as "a city with its back to the sea, built turning in upon itself, like a snail,"[18] is echoed in the conclusion to Rieux's opening overview of the setting for *The Plague*. He calls attention to Oran's "being so disposed that it turns its back on the bay, with the result that it's impossible to see the sea, you always have to go to look for it" (5–6). The city's segregation from the sea is reinforced when an epidemic is declared and the rules of quarantine forbid any residents from wandering to the harbor. It is an extraordinary departure from routine when, late in the book, Rieux and Tarrou violate regulations and sneak off for a brief, exhilarating swim in the sea.

The sea, present or absent, is a crucial image in *The Plague*, and the daily weather and the passage of the seasons neatly mirror the despondency and then burgeoning hope of the people of Oran. Camus's use of these images could easily be dismissed as another humanistic appropriation of the natural world, the projection of human emotions and significations onto the nonhuman environment that the Victorian critic John Ruskin scorned as "the pathetic fallacy." The Camus canon, however, is inconceivable without such naturalistic analogies. In 1958, concluding his retrospective preface to a new edition of essays he had written two decades earlier, Camus noted: "A man's work is nothing but this slow trek to rediscover, through the detours of art, those two or three great and simple images in whose presence his heart first opened."[19]

For Camus, those images were the sea, the sun, and the sky. He grew up by the sea and luxuriated in the sensuality of outdoor life along the Mediterranean shore of Africa. As the essayist of *Nuptials*, he celebrated "this sun, this sea, my heart leaping with youth, the salt taste of my body and this vast landscape in which tenderness and glory merge in blue and yellow."[20] Most of Camus's fiction takes place in a coastal landscape, but when it does not, the mood is especially grim. During his own first visit to Prague, he explains in an essay entitled "Death in the Soul," he "was suffocating, surrounded by walls." It was there, far from his native Mediterranean, that Camus learned "the lesson of the sun and the land I was born in."[21] He chose landlocked Czechoslovakia for the setting of his 1944 play *The Misunderstanding* precisely to emphasize the gloom and doom to which a son returns after many years abroad in a Mediterranean country and in which he finds death at the hands of his own mother and sister. The fact that littoral Oran lies with its back to the sea and, for most of *The Plague*, is denied any access at all to the harbor tantalizes with the thwarted hope of salvation.

9

Paneloux

The Plague is very carefully constructed in five sections, and symmetrically positioned within parts 2 and 4, like twin pillars sustaining the entire edifice, are the two sermons delivered by Father Paneloux. A learned Jesuit whose specialties are ancient inscriptions and Saint Augustine's role in the African Church, Paneloux is widely respected, even by the nondevout (and there are many in Oran), for his doctrinal dedication and fiery eloquence. When Paneloux is scheduled to deliver the culminating sermon during the Week of Prayer called in the early stages of the plague, he draws a large and avid crowd to the city's cathedral. The stocky, bespectacled priest's oration—which he gives on a Sunday at the end of a high mass celebrated under the auspices of Saint Roch, the fourteenth-century patron of plague victims—marks, Rieux contends, "an important date in the history of the period" (85). Paneloux's first sermon compels the Oranians to begin to take the epidemic seriously. Along with the address he gives several months later, it is a crucial device for articulating some of the novel's philosophical themes. And it provides an index to the development of a distinctive character along a wide dramatic arc. Paneloux is not the same in Part 4 as he is in part 2, and neither are most of his fellow citizens. Neither is the reader.

Gazing down at the congregation from the cathedral pulpit, Paneloux begins his address vigorously and directly, with the fervor of the seventeenth-century preacher Jacques-Bénigne Bossuet: "Calamity has come on you, my brethren, and, my brethren, you deserved it" (86–87). While his overflow audience listens in rapt silence, he proceeds to expound on that notion, drawing on biblical allusions and on historical precedents, incidents of plague throughout the world that Camus had studied in his research for the novel. As his words pour forth, a heavy rainfall hits the streets outside, and when he concludes, sunshine has returned to the May Mediterranean morning.

Several crucial elements stand out in Paneloux's sermon. Throughout, he insists on viewing the plague not as some random misfortune or even as a natural biological phenomenon. It is, instead, an instrument of divine retribution. The affliction that Oran is suffering is an enforcement of *lex talionis*, the biblical law of retaliation; it is the scourge of an angry Deity intent on using disease to punish and educate wayward mortals: "For plague is the flail of God and the world his threshing-floor, and implacably He will thresh out His harvest until the wheat is separated from the chaff" (87). Paneloux forcefully describes a universe that is intelligible, in which epidemics can be understood as agents of an elaborate system of rewards and punishments. Like the sermon itself, plague is a didactic tool, and its survivors must open their hearts and heed its lessons: "This same pestilence which is slaying you works for your good and points your path" (90). Like Jonathan Edwards in his famous hellfire sermon, Paneloux characterizes his audience as sinners in the hands of an angry God and depicts God Himself anthropomorphically, as a Being understandable in terms of human emotions like wrath and appeasement. What is equally significant about Paneloux's initial sermon is that, presenting himself as an intermediary of God, he addresses the congregation with the French second-person *vous*—the plural and formal form of "you." As though the plague were their problem and not his, Paneloux's choice of pronouns betrays a psychological and theological detachment from his fellow Oranians.

By the time of his second sermon, in part 4, it is autumn, and the plague has been exacting an enormous toll from the residents of Oran. The audience in the cathedral is now much sparser, not only because the population in general has been winnowed by death but because many have either become skeptical about the value of religion or else embraced apocalyptic superstitions at odds with the Church. When the celebrated preacher speaks now, he begins by stumbling over some of his words, in a tremulous voice and a mournful tone. Paneloux does not exactly repudiate his earlier remarks, but he now proclaims ignorance of God's designs. No longer convinced of the divine logic behind human suffering, he has abandoned his anthropomorphic theology and his belief in an intelligible cosmos. The plague has struck and spared innocents and sinners capriciously, and Paneloux admits he can no longer ascribe to it any rational purpose. Instead, he affirms the need to love God as an irresolvable mystery and to embrace His creation without understanding it. On the brink of what a young deacon, reacting to the sermon on his way out of the cathedral, suggests might be heresy, the Jesuit Paneloux has adopted a position resembling the third-century theologian Tertullian's *credo quia absurdum est*—I believe because it is absurd—a position closer to Camus's own absurdist vision. "My brothers," Paneloux tells his listeners, "the love of God is a hard love. It demands total self-surrender, disdain of our human personality. And yet it alone can reconcile us to suffering and the deaths of children, it alone can justify them, since we cannot understand them, and we can only make God's will ours" (205). But as important as the change in *what* Paneloux says in his second sermon is the shift in *how* he says it: he no longer employs the aloof pronoun *vous* but rather the collaborative *nous*—"we." In a transition that is the converse of Rieux's movement from third-person to first-person, Paneloux has been transformed from an individual commentator into a communal participant.

Apart from the cumulative weariness and frustration of five months of plague, one incident in particular is responsible for Paneloux's dramatic change of heart: the death of Othon's young son Philippe, the description of which provides the most moving passage in the entire novel. As a magistrate, Othon is professionally committed to the logic of rewards and punishments that Paneloux proclaims in his first sermon, and it is understandable that Othon's verdict on that sermon is: "absolutely irrefutable" (92). The magistrate's demeanor is as formal as Paneloux's homiletic style. Tarrou's notebooks record the daily meals that Othon, "a tall, thin man, always dressed in black and wearing a starched collar," takes in a hotel dining room with his wife and two small children. A stern disciplinarian, Othon "uses no terms of endearment to his family, addresses politely spiteful remarks to his wife, and bluntly tells the kids what he thinks of them" (26).

Despite the Othons' strict adherence to the letter of the law, they are suspected of being infected with the plague. In fact, that hardly seems a contradiction, given the initial description of Othon as having something of the air "of an undertaker's assistant" (10) and the suggestion, developed especially through the character of Tarrou, of a link between judgment and death. Mother, father, and daughter are quarantined in a crowded stadium on the outskirts of the city whose inspiration, Camus's notes make clear, was in the Nazi concentration camps. The young son, who is actually afflicted with the disease, is taken to a hospital, where Rieux, in despair of his recovery, decides to test Dr. Castel's new antiplague serum on him. Hour by hour, for five distressing pages of text, a team including Rieux, Tarrou, Rambert, Castel, and Paneloux attends to the boy in his terminal agony:

> They had already seen children die—for many months now death had shown no favoritism—but they had never yet watched a child's agony minute by minute, as they had now been doing since daybreak. Needless to say, the pain inflicted on these innocent victims had always seemed to them to be what in fact it was: an abominable thing. But hitherto they had felt its abomination in, so to speak, an abstract way; they had never had to witness over so long a period the death-throes of an innocent child. (192–193)

Othon *fils* puts up a valiant resistance to the disease, yet the effect of his fortitude is merely to prolong and intensify the unbearable agony. When Philippe does finally die, in excruciating torment, it is difficult to reconcile Paneloux's theory of merited suffering with what he and the others have just witnessed. Anticipating the embrace of divine enigma in his second sermon, Paneloux suggests: "That sort of thing is revolting because it passes our understanding. But perhaps we should love what we cannot understand" (196). Rieux's response is as indignant as he ever gets in *The Plague* and echoes Camus's own endorsement, in his 1951 book *The Rebel,* of revolt, however futile, against the absurd order of things: "No, Father. I've a very different idea of love. And until my dying day I shall refuse to love a scheme of things in which children are put to torture" (196–97).

Through the Othon episode, Camus raises the issue of theodicy— the attempt to reconcile the ways of God to human beings, particularly when those ways entail the prevalence of evil. How can the suffering of an innocent person—as the young Othon, who has not yet had the opportunity to be a sinner, so manifestly is—be explained within a universe governed by the biblical God? According to the traditional definition of God, to which Jesuits and others would be expected to subscribe, the Supreme Being is omniscient, omnipotent, and omnibenevolent; He is all-knowing, all-powerful, and quintessentially good. The horrors of World War II challenged that definition for Camus and for many of those who experienced the Nazi death camps. It is clear that Camus created the figure of the priest Paneloux in order to test the efficacy of traditional religion in a universe perceived as absurd. In a notebook entry during an early stage of writing *The Plague,* Camus imagined a short story about a clergyman whose beliefs are defeated by the reality of death: "A priest, happy with his lot in a country parish in Provence. By accident, has to succor a man sentenced to death just before his execution. Loses his faith because of it."[1]

In the case of Othon's son in *The Plague,* we cannot rationalize his suffering by asserting that God simply was unaware of it, since, being by definition omniscient, God knows absolutely everything. Nor can we dismiss the problem by speculating that God did indeed know about it but was powerless to intervene, since God is omnipotent. Neither can we contend that God knew about the child's agony and could have prevented it but simply refused; a Deity who is all-good would surely not abide the torments of innocent creatures.

What are the individual's ethical responsibilities in a universe of plague? If all is governed by a God whose design accounts for every detail, it would seem senseless to hold human beings accountable for anything, good or bad. Credit and blame both presuppose free will, and it is not clear to what extent human beings are sovereigns of their own fate in either Paneloux's first sermon or his second. If they are not, then humans are more pitiable than culpable. Similarly, as will be seen in Jean Tarrou's ambition to be "a saint without God" (230), a universe that operates either by chance or by impersonal physical forces would seem to leave no latitude for ethics. "How ought we to behave?" becomes an absurd question in a pestilential world devoid of choice, and yet it is a crucial issue in *The Plague*.

The strain of his theodicy accounts for the altered tone and content of Paneloux's second sermon, just as the strain of the collective ordeal ultimately leads to the priest's affliction with an illness whose symptoms are not exactly those of the plague. Refusing to the end to abandon his principles, Paneloux, who had been working on an essay entitled "Is a Priest Justified in Consulting a Doctor?" declines medical assistance and resigns himself to his torturous fever and inevitable death. Rieux's inscription on Paneloux's official document reads: "Doubtful case" (211). But they are all doubtful cases in the world of *The Plague*, where it is not clear that medicine is any more effective than prayer in confronting the absurd.

10

Tarrou

In the post-Nietzschean world that Camus creates, where God is either dead or missing, Jean Tarrou aspires to be "a saint without God" (230). Is it possible to lead an ethical life without the guidance and sanction of an absolute authority, or does the disappearance of a deity lead inevitably to moral anarchy? And in a world contaminated by plague, is it possible not to be implicated in evil? Despite Tarrou's presence throughout the novel, he remains a shadowy figure whose principal function is to raise such thematic questions and to provide Rieux both with additional sources of information for his own text and with the only convincing, though fragile, example of friendship during the plague.

An outsider in Oran who enters enthusiastically into the city's fight against the epidemic, Tarrou keeps extensive journal notes on various oddities he observes, entries that Rieux will later gratefully appropriate for his own chronicle. As a newcomer, Tarrou notices phenomena that natives might take for granted, from a perspective that they would not likely assume. "We might almost imagine," says Rieux, "that Tarrou had a habit of observing events and people through the wrong end of a telescope" (22). More than any of the several other writers within *The Plague*, Tarrou defamiliarizes Oran, is attentive to details and routines of life in the city that Rieux or Grand might take for granted. In fact, he has erected awareness into a central principle of his existence. "How contrive not to waste one's time?" Tarrou asks himself in his diary. "*Answer*: By being fully aware of it all the while" (24). Tarrou's suggestions for achieving this heightened and perpetual awareness—"By spending one's days on an uneasy chair in a dentist's waiting-room; by remaining on one's balcony all a Sunday afternoon; by listening to lectures in a language one doesn't know; by traveling by the longest and least-convenient train routes, and of course standing all the way; by lining up at the box-office of theaters and then not buying a seat" (24–25)—require the kind of disciplined patience with tedium that surviving the plague and reading *The Plague* demand.

Tarrou also represents a figure common to much of Camus's writings: the alien. Indeed, Tarrou is simply a more blatant case of what everyone, regardless of origin, ultimately is. "It is constantly my lot to remain apart," wrote Camus about himself in his own notebook.[1] Tarrou differs from the rest of the people of Oran only in that he recognizes that he is fundamentally alone. We read selections from Tarrou's diary and see him in the company of Rieux, Cottard, Grand, Rambert, Paneloux, and others, but so distracted is everyone by the collective ordeal that it is not until late in part 4 that anyone learns very much about the man's singular background.

In an awkward, ten-page stretch inserted into part 4 just before he and Rieux sneak off for their revivifying swim, Tarrou takes the doctor aside and decides to tell him the story of his life. He explains that he ran away from home at the age of 18 when his father, a prosecuting attorney, took his son to see what he did at work. Horrified and disgusted by the spectacle of a man condemned to death and by his beloved father's role in imposing the maximum penalty, Tarrou could no longer abide living with his parents. He ascribes his loss of innocence to the realization he felt, sitting in the courtroom, of his own complicity in licensed murder. Convinced that "the social order around me was based on the death sentence, and by fighting the established order I'd be fighting against murder," Tarrou became an itinerant foe of the oppressive status quo. "I joined forces with a group of people I then liked, and indeed have never ceased to like. I spent many years in close co-operation with them, and there's not a country in Europe in whose struggles I haven't played a part" (226).

An execution Tarrou witnessed in Hungary, however, struck him with the epiphany that, even in combating organized homicide, he was, albeit unwittingly, colluding with evil, that opposition to tyranny was hopelessly compromised by the very tactics and premises it was contesting. In this very general account, Tarrou is reflecting Camus's own discomfort with those foes of fascism who resorted to violence to achieve their goals. Much to the chagrin of many of his comrades on the left, Camus became as outspoken an anticommunist as he was an antifascist. He forcefully opposed torture and execution in the service of either end of the political spectrum. The title of his first book, the 1937 essay collection *L'Envers et l'endroit* (The Wrong Side and the Right Side), projects Camus's lifelong sense of being torn between opposing choices and factions: solitary and solidary; Algeria and France; the United States and the Soviet Union. Tarrou also anticipates Camus's troubled position during the Algerian war when he criticized the violence on both sides of the conflict. During an abortive attempt to mediate between French colonialists and Arab revolutionaries, he argued that worthy ends are corrupted by homicidal means. Tarrou's refusal to oppose atrocities with additional evil is also a major theme in a 1949 Camus play. *The Just Assassins* dramatizes a cell of revolutionaries in 1905 Russia who are so dedicated to their abstract ideal of justice that some are willing to kill—even innocent children— and be killed in order to attain it. Camus himself was horrified at how atrocious means corrupt our noble ends and refused to ignore the outrages committed by both left and right in the sullied name of freedom. As he proclaimed in the title to a series of articles he published in 1946, in a world of organized violence we must choose to be *"Ni victimes, ni bourreaux"*—neither victims nor executioners. Tarrou is a universalist, equally at home and ill at ease in Oran, Hungary, and wherever anyone is suffering. For Camus, Algeria became the home to which he could never really return, and France was the land in which

he lived, uncomfortably. "Yes, I have a native land: the French language," he confided to his notebook, in characteristically lucid French.[2]

"And thus I came to understand," explains Tarrou, "that I, any-
how, had had plague through all those long years in which, paradoxi-
cally enough, I'd believed with all my soul that I was fighting it. I
learned that I had had an indirect hand in the deaths of thousands of
people; that I'd even brought about their deaths by approving of acts
and principles which could only end that way" (227). And so, weary
of contributing to moral pestilence as part of any party and committed
now to the simple tenet "that on this earth there are pestilences and
there are victims, and it's up to us, so far as possible, not to join forces
with the pestilences" (229), he casts his lot with the victims. Tarrou
happens to show up, alone, in Oran just a few weeks before the city's
rats begin dying and the health authorities proclaim an epidemic.

In his revulsion from judicial brutality, society's elaborately camouflaged pretext for oppression, Tarrou serves to dramatize further
the novel's critique of a talionic legalistic system based exclusively on
rewards and punishments. "I believe in justice," declared Camus at a
1957 press conference in Stockholm, where he had gone to accept the
Nobel Prize, "but I shall defend my mother above justice."[3] Tarrou,
who is also partial to mothers—his own and Rieux's—extends the
preoccupation with the abstractness and capriciousness of justice that
Camus had brought earlier to *The Stranger*, the 1942 novel whose first
half recounts events leading up to a gratuitous murder and whose
second depicts the trial and execution of the defendant, Meursault.
Tarrou also anticipates the character of Jean-Baptiste Clamence, the
self-styled "judge-penitent" whose rambling discourse on universal
guilt constitutes the text of Camus's 1956 novel *The Fall*. Conscious
of his own unworthiness, Tarrou is aware that, if we are to base our
judgments exclusively on merit, no one will escape the firing squad.
Tarrou is much more sympathetic to the sentiments in Paneloux's
second sermon, on love, than to those in his first, on divine retribution.
Behind his back, Tarrou calls Othon "Enemy Number One" (134).
But fascinated by the pater familias magistrate, perhaps a reminder of
his own father, he pities the man when he loses his son and is obliged

to move to a quarantine camp. "One would like to do something to help him," he tells Rambert. "But how can you help a judge?" (219). In place of judgment, Tarrou would substitute a more modest strategy to contend with evil, what he calls "the path of sympathy" (230). It is on that path that Tarrou takes the initiative in organizing the "sanitary squads" that enforce prophylactic measures against the plague in Oran. He himself is a casualty of the battle, one of the final victims of the pestilence that he believes is, at least metaphorically, universal and inescapable.

Tarrou recognizes that combat against the plague can itself be pestiferous. As leader of the sanitary squads, he recognizes that he has enormous power over whether to remove victims from their houses and consign them to quarantine camps and a dubious future. It is in effect the power of life and death, a power that, if exercised irresponsibly, can be as unjust as the pestilence itself, or as those members of the Resistance whom Camus faulted for adopting the same capricious, inhuman tactics as their enemy. Convinced that we all suffer from the plague, Tarrou cautions: "We must keep endless watch on ourselves lest in a careless moment we breathe in somebody's face and fasten the infection on him" (229). The distinction between fighting the plague and spreading it is, for Tarrou, a very subtle one.

Tarrou's uncompromising lucidity as a diarist and his self-sacrifice as a health worker endear him to Rieux, who takes Tarrou into his own house to nurse the newcomer to Oran through his final agony. The alliance between Tarrou and Rieux is a test of whether it is possible to base a relationship on total honesty and of whether that relationship can survive in a pestilential world. It cannot. "For there is no denying," says Rieux, "that the plague had gradually killed off in all of us the faculty not of love only but even of friendship" (165). It comes as no surprise when Camus kills off Tarrou near the novel's end. "There can be no peace without hope," Rieux muses immediately after his friend's death, "and Tarrou, denying as he did the right to condemn anyone whomsoever—though he knew well that no one can help condemning and it befalls even the victim sometimes to turn executioner—Tarrou had lived a life riddled with contradictions and had never known hope's solace" (263). But it is a life that Rieux reveres, and regrets.

Tarrou

Convivial and candid, Tarrou is an attractive figure, one who, like an incarnation of Stoical philosophy, is simultaneously of the world and free of it: "Good-humored, always ready with a smile, he seemed an addict of all normal pleasures without being their slave" (22). If Grand is the story's hero and Rieux its chronicler, Tarrou comes as close as possible to being its saint without God.

Like Camus himself, for whom he is an idealized spokesman, Tarrou is fond of swimming. "An Athenian proverb put the man who could neither read nor swim in the very lowest class of citizens," observed Camus, who was partial to both, in his notebook.[4] More important, Tarrou articulates more directly than any other character in the Camus canon the author's longtime aversion to torture and capital punishment. The depiction of Tarrou's alienation from his revolutionary comrades after witnessing a firing squad in Hungary surely owes some of its feeling to the fact that Camus—who credited his decision to join the Resistance to his horror over the Nazi execution of a prominent French Communist—antagonized many allies in the Resistance when he refused to endorse the execution of Nazi collaborators, however heinous their crimes. He was anxious to find a middle course between the two superpowers of the cold war, whom he regarded as both guilty of institutionalized murder. Later, Camus would alienate himself from both sides of the Algerian conflict when he opposed both French oppression and Arab terrorism.

Camus saw himself as part of the French tradition of committed intellectuals who, like Montaigne, Voltaire, Hugo, and Zola, campaigned to save individuals from violence by the state. In 1957 he published an essay, "Reflections on the Guillotine," that begins with a personal anecdote, one of the few things Camus ever knew about his father. He recalls that, after awakening early one morning eager to attend the execution of a heinous murderer, his father rushed home, sickened by the bloody spectacle, and vomited. The incident, recounted to Camus by his mother, was transformed into Tarrou's prosecutor father's custom of rising early to attend executions and Tarrou's own revulsion over the reality that lay behind his father's work. He is particularly struck by the memory of the firing squad he witnessed in Hungary: "Do you know," he asks Rieux, "that if the victim took two steps forward his chest would touch the rifles? Do you know that, at this short range, the soldiers concentrate their fire on the region of the heart and their big bullets make a hole into which you could thrust your fist?" (227). "There will be no enduring peace in either individual hearts or social transactions as long as the death penalty is not outlawed," declares Camus at the conclusion of "Reflections on the Guillotine," a reasoned and impassioned screed against capital punishment.[5] Camus's arguments against execution and other injustices do not rely solely on personal revulsion, though he makes no effort to conceal his own horror at legalized murder. Employing an epidemiological metaphor reminiscent of *The Plague*, he declares that capital punishment "is to the body politic what cancer is to the individual body, with this difference: no one has ever spoken of the necessity of cancer."[6] But Camus is careful to construct a logical case against the guillotine based on the fallibility of juridical decisions and the ineffectiveness of physical termination as a deterrent.

In a 1948 response to Emmanuel d'Astier's attack on his essay "Neither Victims nor Executioners," Camus acknowledges that violence cannot be eliminated from human life:

> Violence is both inevitable and unjustifiable. I believe that it is necessary to keep regarding it as exceptional and to push it back within whatever limits we can. I thus preach neither non-violence, of whose impossibility I am all too aware, nor, despite the scoffers, sainthood; I know myself too well to believe in pure virtue. But in a world where terror is rationalized by arguments on both sides, I think that it is necessary to impose a limit on violence, to sequester it when it is inevitable, blunt its terrifying effects by preventing it from reaching the full force of its wrath.

Critics ridiculed Camus for crediting Tarrou with the ambition to be a saint without God, insinuating that the author himself maintained such pompous aspirations. But despite his evident embarrassment here over the project of sainthood, it is clear that Camus shares Tarrou's abhorrence of violence, whether administered by the state or as a consequence of clever theories. "I am horrified," Camus continues, "by those whose words outrun their acts. It is in that that I distance myself from some of our great minds, whose calls for murder I will cease to despise when they hold the rifles of the firing squad themselves."[7] In his empathy for victims and his unyielding opposition to assassination through abstraction, Tarrou was created in the image of his maker.

There is another writer whose attitudes and actions resemble those of Tarrou and Camus. George Orwell was also an implacable foe of totalitarianisms of the right and the left alike. Both authors died prematurely, at 46, and attracted veritably cultish veneration. Like Camus, who was ten years his junior, Orwell turned from journalism to fiction, insisting in both on a style that was lucid and accessible. "All our troubles," contends Tarrou, "spring from our failure to use plain, clean-cut language" (230). The statement, made in the midst of a murderous plague, might seem hyperbolic, an example of an author erecting his own preoccupation with the niceties of style into a universal principle. How could all the sorrows of the world spring from vapid jargon and dangling participles? What do the obsessions of Tarrou, Grand, and Rieux about putting the right word in the right place have to do with fighting the plague?

In his 1946 essay "Politics and the English Language," an impassioned plea for the values of lucidity, common sense, and honesty, Orwell suggests an answer. Bemoaning the infection of modern English with euphemisms, clichés, pompous diction, and empty verbiage, and the use of words not to communicate but to obfuscate, Orwell argues that "if thought corrupts language, language can also corrupt thought." We think through language, and a language that no longer permits clarity and honesty prevents us from confronting and combating the problems of the world, becomes itself a major problem. If, according to Orwell, "politics itself is a mass of lies, evasions, folly, hatred and schizophrenia," it is because we have abandoned a clear style and hence clear thoughts.[8] Orwell—like Tarrou and Camus—believed that we are what we say, and if our language has become confused, inert, or deceitful, so, too, have we. Orwell dramatizes this principle in *Nineteen Eighty-Four* (1949) in the use of Newspeak, the official language of Big Brother's Oceania, where war is peace, freedom is slavery, ignorance is strength, and the individual has thereby lost the capacity for honest and independent analysis. Newspeak is the natural medium of tyranny; in fact, it offers no alternative. In a footnote to *The Rebel*, Camus concurs: "It is worth noting that the language peculiar to totalitarian doctrines is always a scholastic or administrative language." On the same page, he contends: "Every ambiguity, every misunderstanding, leads to death; clear language and simple words are the only salvation from this death."[9]

"Good prose is like a window pane," wrote Orwell in the fine prose of a 1947 essay, "Why I Write," that parallels Camus's preoccupation with economy and directness of expression, with writing that is transparent, if not white.[10] In a 1944 tribute to the philosopher Brice Parain, Camus noted that "Parain's basic idea is one of honesty: the criticism of language cannot get around the fact that our words commit us and that we should remain faithful to them. Naming an object inaccurately means adding to the unhappiness of this world."[11] Like Parain, Orwell, and Camus, Tarrou is scornful of ideologues who camouflage their murderous intent behind specious slogans and intimidating blather. The misuse of language is another instance of that abstraction, that refusal to be attentive to the tiny truths of experience, represented by the cruelly grandiose political systems of our century and by the plague. Big Brother could not dominate a society that used Tarrou's plain, clear-cut language. If Faulkner and Proust might disappear from such a world, so, too, would Hitler and Stalin.

Averse to personal flamboyance in a way that Rieux can only envy, Tarrou was born to disappear. "One can write nothing readable unless one constantly struggles to efface one's own personality," wrote George Orwell, the literary personality who replaced the man who was born as Eric Blair.[12] Like an exceedingly unprepossessing Lone Ranger, Tarrou, masking much of his identity, arrives mysteriously in Oran to help its citizens fight an evil foe. Almost as self-effacing as Rieux's mother, he completes his work and, during a long night of silence, departs Oran through death. But he leaves behind a journal and the memory of his example as an inspiration to Rieux and the other survivors. Both the life and the writings are plain, clear-cut, and saintly in a secular way.

11

Cottard

"There is but one truly serious philosophical problem, and that is suicide," declares Camus in the opening sentence of *The Myth of Sisyphus*.[1] We first encounter Cottard, a plump little man, in the aftermath of a thwarted attempt to hang himself. His neighbor, Joseph Grand, has cut him down just in time from a makeshift noose and called on Rieux for help. Despite his try at suicide, Cottard is not exactly a philosopher, though his life after the aborted hanging does raise important philosophical questions about individual identity and social responsibility. Cottard is a man driven to take desperate measures by the fear that he is about to be arrested for an unspecified crime he committed several years before. With the outbreak of plague, Cottard is revitalized. The authorities are too distracted by the public health emergency to bother with him, and Cottard exploits the crisis for private gain. He takes advantage of the quarantine to profit in contraband, making a small fortune by selling smuggled cigarettes and liquor.

From being sullen and withdrawn, Cottard becomes gregarious and cheerful during the plague. "He is blossoming out," records Tarrou's diary. "Expanding in geniality and good humor" (174). Cottard is an opportunist, and the city's misfortune provides him with the opportunity to enrich himself. Aside from the minor underworld figures Garcia, Gonzales, Marcel, and Louis whom Rambert solicits in his scheme to escape from Oran, Cottard is the only egoist among the characters in *The Plague*. Part 3 makes passing reference to unnamed Oranians who take advantage of vacated houses to loot them, but Cottard is the only major figure who does not in some way volunteer in the communal effort against the ravages of disease.

For a while, Raymond Rambert, a young journalist for one of the leading dailies in Paris who happens to find himself in Oran at the outbreak of the plague, is tempted into making a separate peace, into abandoning the city to its collective combat. "I don't belong here!" (77), he exclaims to Rieux, pleading with the doctor to help him find a way out of Oran. Faced with the horror of plague, Rambert is initially as evasive as the dozens of New Yorkers who, in the notorious Kitty Genovese case, witnessed a rape and murder outside their apartment windows and failed even to call the police, claiming they "did not want to get involved." "Short, square-shouldered, with a determined-looking face and keen, intelligent eyes" (11), Rambert makes elaborate, illicit arrangements to avoid involvement in the problems of Oran. He prefers to pursue his personal happiness by returning to his woman in Paris. But Rambert's is a farewell to arms that is not endorsed by Camus and that he himself eventually rejects. Demystifying the romantic celebration of couples who gladly renounce the world for love, Rambert recognizes that "it may be shameful to be happy by oneself" (188). Choosing the misery of company, Rambert stays in Oran and throws himself into the communal struggle against the plague.

But Cottard stands apart. He even welcomes the calamity because it provides him with personal reprieve from arrest and profit from the black market. Invited by Tarrou to join his sanitary squads, Cottard replies: "It's not my job." He alone of Rieux's characters is proud to be alone. Cottard adds: "What's more, the plague suits me quite well and I see no reason why I should bother about trying to stop it" (145). The plague also induces in Cottard, however, a curious feeling of solidarity. Fear of arrest has isolated him. But wracked by guilt and the dread of being held accountable for an earlier, undefined misdeed, Cottard exults in the ability to lose himself amid the general ordeal. He takes to frequenting cafés, restaurants, dance halls, and other public places and becomes anxious for the good opinion of others, hopeful of recruiting them to bear witness to his redeeming traits. Cottard is an egoist desperate for endorsement by others, one who, like Jean-Baptiste Clamence in *The Fall*, is never so elated over his isolation as when he can share the elation with someone else. Tarrou, who himself claims to have been suffering from "the plague" long before he encountered the infectious bacillus, observes that Cottard was in effect a plague victim before the onset of the epidemic and that the adversities of the rest of Oran now at last put them all in the same situation.

> In short, this epidemic has done him proud. Of a lonely man who hated loneliness it has made an accomplice. Yes, "accomplice" is the word that fits, and doesn't he relish his complicity! He is happily at one with all around him, with their superstititions, their groundless panics, the susceptibilities of people whose nerves are always on the stretch; with their fixed idea of talking the least possible about plague and nevertheless talking of it all the time; with their abject terror at the slightest headache, now they know headache to be an early symptom of the disease; and lastly, with their frayed, irritable sensibility that takes offense at trifling oversights and brings tears to their eyes over the loss of a trouser-button. (176)

It is hard not to see in Cottard a portrait of the collaborationist, those French who gained advantage by cooperating with the tyrants of World War II rather than resisting them. The Nazi sympathizers who flourished under the puppet regime of Marshal Henri Philippe Pétain were a disgrace to French ideals of liberty and equality. However, in part because we see him through the eyes of Tarrou and Rieux, who try to be nonjudgmental and are almost as antagonistic toward police as the black marketeer is, Cottard emerges as a remarkably sympathetic character. Tarrou's verdict, which provokes an immediate urge for absolution, is that Cottard is forgivably guilty: "His only real crime is that of having in his heart approved of something that killed off men, women, and children. I can understand the rest, but for *that*

I am obliged to pardon him" (272). In the agnostic theology that underlies *The Plague*, we are all guilty of original sin. Like Tarrou and more than most others, Cottard recognizes this and sees in the plague a demonstration of the universal imperfection of the human condition. Cottard is an overly resourceful entrepreneur, but unlike the many French guilty of criminal collaboration during the 1940s, he does nothing actively to bring about the torture, confinement, or death of his fellow citizens. At worst, he can be accused of aquiescing in horror, of refusing to take steps to fight it, though under Nazi domination such steps were often counterproductive, when Resistance sabotage provoked retaliation against innocent hostages. Under the tyranny of Camus's plague, those steps seem utterly irrelevant to the outcome of an epidemic that eludes human control and understanding. Illegal but not flagrantly antisocial, Cottard's activities during the quarantine are a paradoxical affirmation of an egoist's complicity with his fellow citizens. He elicits the sympathetic understanding of an author who refused to participate in the orgy of vengeance against collaborators that followed the liberation of France from Nazi tyranny. Even after Cottard becomes homicidally deranged after the lifting of the plague, Camus, who incurred the wrath of his Resistance comrades for opposing the execution of collaborators, refuses to have Rieux condemn him. "What is the ideal of the man who is a prey to the plague?" Camus asked himself in his notebook. His reply: "I'm certainly going to make you laugh: it's honesty [*l'honnêteté*]."[2] Cottard's behavior during the plague falls far short of the ideal. He is dishonest, but he nevertheless elicits the sympathy of the nonjudgmental Tarrou and Rieux.

As the plague begins to abate, Cottard's mood alters dramatically, though he tries to cling to some hope that the remission is either illusory or temporary. When police officers come to question him, he runs off into the darkness. Our final glimpse of Cottard occurs after the quarantine has been lifted. A screaming maniac, he is being carried off by brutal police. They had surrounded his house and succeeded in taking him captive after Cottard, gone berserk, had begun shooting at the joyous crowds congregating in the street to celebrate the end of the plague. He manages to wound one civilian and one policeman and to kill a hapless spaniel who strays into his line of fire. But even at the end of the book, Cottard is not guilty of a capital offense but of the ineradicable and ambiguous charge of being human. Neither Camus nor Tarrou would recommend the guillotine. Cottard's own despair is severe enough a punishment.

12

Absences

It is an eventful year in Oran, but *The Plague* is organized less around incidents than a series of conversations among half a dozen characters. The novel's plot, the passage of an epidemic from outbreak to blatancy to latency, is less inventive and less important to Camus's purposes than the creation of memorable characters, and those characters are constructed primarily to articulate the novel's themes. It is a tribute to the economy of Camus's artistry that *The Plague* succeeds in suggesting the density of a busy port city by sketching in only a few human figures. Analysis of the novel's characters is analysis of the novel, because those characters are carefully chosen to represent the full range of reactions to the plague that interest Camus.

However, major omissions haunt the cast of characters. It is extraordinary that a story set in Algeria's second largest city should have so entirely ignored a fundamental segment of its population. By 1990, three decades after the conclusion of its bloody and successful struggle for independence from France, Algeria had outlawed the use of French for official purposes. Yet nowhere in *The Plague* is there a single character who speaks Arabic, and certainly none who speaks a Berber tongue. Islam, which is now the state religion of Algeria, has no place in the novel. For those of Camus's characters who are religious at all, there is indeed one God; He is not Allah, however, but rather the Deity of the Roman Catholic church. All of Camus's characters are either *colons*—descendants of the French Europeans who took control of North Africa in the early nineteenth century or of the Spanish who had established a foothold earlier—or Europeans.

Though the plague in Oran is a municipal emergency and collective measures are organized through official channels, Camus's novel remains vague about the political organization of the Algerian city. Government actions seem exclusively local, initiated independently of Paris by Francophonic men whose authority is neither accounted for nor questioned. The highest official in Oran remains anonymous, referred to merely as "the Prefect." Use of the majusculed generic title instead of a proper name is less suggestive of a faceless tyrant, a Maghreb Big Brother, than of the detached, ineffectual bureaucrat he appears to be at every meeting. Colonialism is less significant in an analysis of Oran's power structure than is epidemiology; the plague is mightier than the state.

Though the names of the underworld characters Garcia and Gonzalez reflect the influence of Spain on Algeria, by conquest in the fifteenth century and through commerce later, Camus's Oranians are exclusively Francophonic and largely extensions of French culture. Although Joseph Grand comes from Montélimar in southern France, the fiftyish municipal clerk has apparently lived in Oran for most of his life. Nevertheless, the sentence he is writing is about the Bois de Boulogne, a park in Paris. Raymond Rambert has come from Paris, on assignment to investigate health conditions among the Arabs, but he abandons that mission before he even begins. The outbreak of the plague presumably puts an end to Rambert's research, though why it should is not clear. Camus himself, who was sent to Oran in 1939 by the newspaper *Alger-Républicain* to investigate a case of collusion by the colonialist elite and wealthy landowners against poorer farmers and consumers, stayed to complete his assignment. He wrote a series of articles exposing injustice in the trial of Michel Hodent, a government official who had opposed attempts to manipulate the price of wheat. As a journalist caught in Oran, Rambert has a sensational scoop, and he ought to be able to telegraph to his editor exclusive accounts of the effect of plague on the Arab population as well as on the rest of Oran. Yet even after he abandons his scheme to escape the quarantine, Rambert neglects his assignment and, as far as we can tell, remains oblivious to the plight of the city's Arabs during the plague. So, more remarkably, does Rieux, and the reader does not encounter one Arab in all five parts of *The Plague*. It is true that in the 1940s, before the drive toward independence stimulated a large-scale exodus of Algeria's *colons* to metropolitan France, Arabs constituted only a minority of Oran's population. A 1938 study, René Lespès' *Oran: Etude de géographie et d'histoire urbaine* (Oran: A Study of Urban Geography and History), described Oran as "the most 'European' city of Algeria,"[1] but the 23.7 percent of Oranians who nevertheless were Arab are absent from *The Plague*.

Arabs exist in the novel as little more than a rumor. Grand and Cottard are in a tobacco shop one day when the owner begins gossiping about a recent murder case in Algiers: "A young commercial employee had killed an Algerian on a beach" (51). In fact, the original French text specifies that the victim is an *Arab*: "*I'll s'agissait d'un jeune employé de commerce qui avait tué un Arabe sur une plage*" (1262). Those are the only details we learn about the incident, which is in effect a précis of the plot of Camus's 1942 novel *The Stranger*. It is a metafictional moment, as if the prattling tobacconist in *The Plague* were stepping outside the story to analyze an earlier text, in which the fictional Meursault kills a man on the beach who, for all his importance to the plot, is never identified except as "an Arab." Arabs are invisible characters in Camus's North African writings, but it is less a matter of rabid racism than of his pied-noirs feeling like strangers in their own homeland. His most widely anthologized short story, "L'Hôte" (1957) which could be translated as either "The Guest" or the "The Host," is in fact a mockery of hospitality. Daru, schoolmaster in a remote Algerian settlement, finds himself alienated both from the European culture he is assigned to teach and from the indigenous people who are identified merely as "Arabs." Neither comfortable with the colonialist oppressors nor accepted by the resentful Arabs, he is yet another variation on the Camus outsider. Daru frees an Arab rebel he was ordered to deliver to prison, but the gesture is misinterpreted by the other Arabs. "In this vast landscape he had loved so much, he was alone," concludes "The Guest."[2] Rieux, too, is alone, and his solitude is compounded by the fact that Oran's Arabs remain absent from his text.

So, too, do its Jews. Camus originally considered setting part of *The Plague* in the city's Jewish quarter, but the idea did not survive the finished text. Married at a time of virulent anti-Semitism and even genocide to a woman, Francine, who was part Jewish, Camus was acutely sensitive to the fate of the Jews in modern history. When he began his research into the incidence of plagues, he noted again and again the cruel way in which Jews were blamed for the depradations of the Black Death in medieval Europe, how they were slaughtered as scapegoats in an attempt to purge a community of its impurities. The detention camps for those afflicted with the plague in Oran are modeled after the Nazi concentration camps for removing non-Aryans. Nevertheless, although any contemporary reader could be expected to sense the parallels, the characters in the final version of *The Plague* are leached of any Jewish identity. Camus was most intent on envisioning a world in which ethnicity is irrelevant, in which all are victims. While such abstractions might serve a metaphysical purpose, in social contexts victimization is often a direct function of ethnicity. In an actual Oran, the presence of Arabs, Jews, or Zulus would not be an incidental detail. Camus's Oran seems devoid of mosques and synagogues, and though the city does contain a cathedral—the site of crucial scenes in parts 2 and 4—its rites remain so nondenominational that it might almost pass for a philosopher's classroom. In Camus's unreal city, ethnic and religious distinctions have disappeared.

For all practical purposes, so, too, have women. "*The Plague*: a world without women and thus suffocating," wrote Camus in his notebook in 1946. Camus wrote much of *The Plague* isolated in France from his wife in Algeria. Many of Camus's diary entries from this period reflect on the celibacy that a wartime isolation was forcing on a man who was fond of philandering. Though seclusion in rural France forced him into a temporary sexual quarantine, Camus maintained relations before and after with several women aside from his wife. Nevertheless, in classifying all authors qua authors as either husbands (reliable, decent, intelligible, and generous) or lovers (exciting, unpredictable, and demanding), Susan Sontag judged Camus the writer to be "the ideal husband of contemporary letters."[3] *The Plague* is poignant with the pangs of separation, but it is also diminished by the want of women.

Like Camus's Francine, who returned to Oran for the start of the school term while her husband remained in Le Panelier to recuperate from tuberculosis, Rieux's wife, who is never identified by name, leaves Oran, never to return, shortly before the outbreak of the plague. Rambert's predicament is highlighted by the fact that the quarantine keeps him from returning to the anonymous woman he loves in Paris. Grand is still in love with Jeanne, but the closest he gets to his estranged wife is to write her a letter in the final moments of the novel. Cottard has to do without women, explains Tarrou, because of "that ugly mug of his" (176). In the opera within the chronicle, Orpheus loses Eurydice before losing his own life to the plague. The magistrate's wife does make occasional appearances within the story, but she is a minor, submissive character, referred to, even by her husband, as "Madame Othon."

Camus projects a world of solitary men—Rieux, Tarrou, Cottard, Rambert, Grand—for whom the presence of active, vibrant women would be a denial of the grim isolation that is their condition under the plague. The separation of lovers that is his obsessive theme is imagined by the bereaved Rieux primarily as a matter of leaving men without women. What tenuous relations *The Plague* does encompass are basically the bonding of man with man: the male camaraderie of Rieux and Tarrou, Marcel and Louis, or the physicians who conspire to fight the epidemic. With the exception of brief mention of the reunion of the elderly Castels, *The Plague* depicts a world of men without women, while no relationship between a woman and a woman is depicted or even imagined. Not merely a matter of sexual frustration, the reintegration of women into the life of Oran would mark the end of the plague. For Rieux, women represent the promise of overcoming man's, and men's, fundamental isolation. They offer the possibility of social cohesion and love. And, of course, Rieux never recovers his woman.

Bernard Rieux's mother, never identified except as "Madame Rieux," plays an important part in the story; but she remains a tenebrous presence, as though maternal love were almost as elusive as the conjugal kind. At one point, in fact, she seems to Tarrou to be "no more than a darker patch of shadow" (259). The day after Rieux's wife leaves for a sanatorium in the mountains, his mother materializes at the apartment to keep house for him—as though he were incapable of doing it himself and domestic labor had to be performed by one woman or another. We learn of no woman active in the public campaign against the plague. The elder Madame Rieux remains at home and is a quiet source of strength for the men who go out to do battle against the disease. Her chores done, she sits in a corner of the living room gazing out the window, her faced filled with "the silent resignation that a laborious life had given it" (112). Madame Rieux *mère* is almost a kind of Algerian Buddha, a figure of ancient serenity amid the turbulence of life and death outside.

She exerts an especial appeal to Tarrou, whom she convinces her son to take into the apartment during his fatal illness. Tarrou devotes the final pages of his diary to details about Madame Rieux, noting "Mme. Rieux's self-effacement, her way of explaining things in the simplest possible words, her predilection for a special window at which she always sat in the early evening, holding herself rather straight, her hands at rest, her eyes fixed on the quiet street below, until twilight filled the room and she showed among the gathering shadows as a motionless black form which gradually merged into the invading darkness" (248). This ideal of self-effacement into invisibility will, of course, also inspire Rieux's efforts as chronicler. Madame Rieux serves as Tarrou's faithful, selfless nurse throughout his final agony. She is a surrogate for his own long-suffering mother, whom Tarrou exempted from the contempt he felt for his magistrate father and whom he took to live with him until her death eight years earlier. Tarrou's final diary entry makes precisely that connection: "She reminds me of my mother; what I loved most in Mother was her self-effacement, her 'dimness,' as they say, and it's she I've always wanted to get back to" (248).

She is similar to another woman in *The Plague*, the mother of Marcel and Louis, the smugglers who offer to sneak Rambert past the city gates. As part of the scheme, Rambert moves in with the two brothers and their mother, who, despite rationing, cooks a fine dish of rice. Of Spanish background, the smugglers' mother is, like Rieux's, silent and supportive. "She was a dried-up little wisp of a woman, always dressed in black, busy as a bee, and she had a nut-brown, wrinkled face and immaculately white hair. No great talker, she merely smiled genially when her eyes fell on Rambert" (183). Her sole recorded conversation is a succinct exchange with Rambert about his Paris woman in which she employs a minimum of words to reveal wise insights into human motivation.

In one of his earliest journal entries, as summarized by Rieux, Tarrou notes "the color of Mme. Rieux's, the doctor's mother's eyes, a limpid brown, and makes the odd observation that a gaze revealing so much goodness of heart would always triumph over plague" (107). *The Plague* sentimentalizes women as self-sacrificing embodiments of tenderness and goodness, and their absence from Camus's Oran emphasizes the privation that infected men must suffer. Like Ernest Hemingway and André Malraux, Camus was sometimes attacked during his own lifetime for portraying a world of men without women, for his inability to create convincingly visible female characters. A gulf of misunderstanding forever separates men and women, and his reader is usually stranded on the virile side of the gulf, not least in Camus's 1944 play *The Misunderstanding*, in which woman's otherness is not so benign: a returning prodigal son is unwittingly murdered by his greedy mother and sister. In *The Myth of Sisyphus*, Don Juan is celebrated as a paragon of absurdist heroism. The Camus novels are stories of male bonding for which female figures are superfluous. In a 1959 interview with Jean-Claude Brisville, during the last year of his life, Camus claimed that his three favorite creations were Marie and Céleste from *The Stranger* and Dora from *The Just Assassins*.[4] But they are minor figures, and he was aware of his shortcomings in the representation of women's experience. In his next book, he intended to render more fully life in North Africa, for its women and men. Yet the manuscript remained unfinished at his death, and its working title was *Le Premier Homme*—The First Man.

A cosmic jest in the form of an automobile accident, in a fast car driven by his publisher, Michel Gallimard, left Camus's work unfinished. But the completed text of *The Plague* is diminished by another absence, of a quality rather than a character. A dissertation on humor in this novel would have to be as terse as the telegrams sent into and out of Oran. Joseph Grand, though, is a genuinely comic creation, an endearing self-mockery by an author sensitive to the manias of his métier. With his zealous dedication to a ludicrous sentence, Grand provides comic relief from the rigors of the plague. So, too, do the bedridden asthmatic who passes his peas and, at least in the beginning, before they contract plague, the fastidious Othons sternly minding their p's and q's.

There is nothing very funny, however, about anyone else, particularly Rieux, Tarrou, Rambert, and Paneloux. They are exceedingly earnest figures, as though mirth were the first casualty of the collective calamity. Saints apparently are not jesters. "Nobody laughs," writes Tarrou in his notebook, "except the drunks, and they laugh too much" (109). Oran, which Rieux at one point describes as "a huge necropolis" (155), could not be confused with an amusement park. In his 1959 interview, Jean-Claude Brisville asked Camus: "Is there in your work a theme that is important to you that you believe to have been neglected by your critics?" Camus's one-word answer was: "Humor."[5] *The Fall* is rich in sardonic wit, but it is hard to credit much humor to most of Camus's other work, particularly *The Plague*.

After his quick recovery from suicidal depression, Cottard is, for the duration of the plague, a figure of cheerful exuberance. When, for example, a man afflicted with the plague rushes out into the street and flings himself on the first woman he encounters, Cottard reacts with glee. "Good for him!" is his spirited comment (74). But in his tone as in much else, Cottard defies the novel's moral norm, by which wisecracks are at variance with wisdom. There is something almost blasphemous about Cottard's delight amid disorder, as if anything but dolor is a sacrilege against the sufferings of Oran. It is true that an occasional wry irony tinges the sentences of Rieux, as when he drolly observes: "At Oran, as elsewhere, for lack of time and thinking, people have to love one another without knowing much about it" (5). Later, through represented discourse, Rieux records the fatuous insouciance of the social elite who gather at the Municipal Opera House: "In the soft hum of well-mannered conversation they regained the confidence denied them when they walked the dark streets of the town; evening dress was a sure charm against plague" (179). The joke is on them, as formal evening dress is, of course, no such thing. "My whole work is ironic," wrote Camus, the laureate of detachment and alienation, in his notebook on 4 March 1950.[6] But for the most part, stylistic charm, much less humor, is not abundant in either the plague or *The Plague*.

Under the ideal of sober veracity endorsed by most of the main characters, particularly Rieux, comedy becomes a dangerous, frivolous diversion from the important tasks at hand. Just as love and friendship have no place in the world of the plague, so, too, does humor seem expendable, indecorous, and even indecent so long as corpses continue to accrue. *The Plague* lacks the black humor that enlivens Kafka's similarly bleak visions of an unfriendly universe. Its style, Rieux's attempt at characterless prose, is designed as a perfect instrument for representing and responding to the gravity of the situation. Lacking the leaven of humor, it veers into sententiousness, its characters into prigs. Humor in *The Plague* is as scarce as the contraband that mischievous Cottard smuggles past the border police. Its sparseness reinforces the grimness of the epidemic and forces the reader, dutifully navigating the solemn prose, to share the hardships of Oran. But it also restricts the range of human possibility, which is an inevitable reality during times of plague, and constricts the repertoire of human expression, which is not.

Happiness, too, is most notable in *The Plague* by its absence. During the quarantine of Oran, rare moments of happiness are tentative, provisional, and fragile—Rieux's and Tarrou's revivifying swim in the sea, Cottard's café bonhommie, couples glimpsed clutching at each other in an embrace to defy death. And even in these, happiness seems defined negatively, as a relief from oppression, more than as positive bliss. In a 1951 notebook entry, Camus recorded his response to a questionnaire asking authors to list their ten favorite words. He cited: "the world, suffering, the earth, the mother, men, the desert, honor, misery, summer, the sea." Most of these are patently key terms in the conception of *The Plague* if not his other works. Conspicuously missing, however, is the one word that, according to Germaine Brée, represented Camus's "essential concern and need."[7] The word is *happiness*, and its omission, like that of *love*, from the author's list—as though it would be fatuous and presumptuous to stake a claim to what, in an absurd universe, can never be attained—is as disturbing as its absence from the fiction Camus created. In the world of *The Plague*, happiness is the obsessive universal desire nowhere attained. The novel's plot, style, and tone are shaped by a futile human quest for absent happiness. "But what is happiness," asks Camus in his *Nuptials* essay "The Desert," "except the simple harmony between a man and the life he leads?"[8] The epidemic in Oran disrupts such harmony. Echoing Edgar Allan Poe, a 1939 entry in Camus's notebook lists "the four conditions for happiness" as: "(1) Life in the open air. (2) The love of another being. (3) Freedom from all ambition. (4) Creation."[9] The advent of plague obliterates all four conditions for happiness. One can only, defiantly, *imagine* Sisyphus happy.

13

The Author and His Work

"I am just grateful to the Nobel Committee for having decided to honor a French writer from Algeria," Albert Camus told a reporter in 1957. "I have never written anything that was not connected, in one way or another, to the land where I was born."[1] The Nobel laureate was born in Algeria in 1913, when the North African country was still administered as part of France, and he died two years before the end of a bitter, bloody struggle that culminated in its independence. Though Camus is usually read and studied as a Frenchman, as the compatriot of Jean-Paul Sartre and André Gide and the heir to the classicism of Jean Racine and Madame de Lafayette that he so admired, he must also be understood as a pied-noir, the descendant of Europeans who settled in the Maghreb after France conquered it in 1830. Camus was not an Arab, but neither was he a native Parisian, and an understanding of his career is incomplete without recognition of his kinship to such other North African Francophones of European descent as Gabriel Audisio, Max-Pol Fouchet, Jean Grenier, Emmanuel Roblès, and Jules Roy. Camus shared his character Father Paneloux's interest in another North African writer, Saint Augustine. The southern Mediterranean landscape of sea, sun, sky, and sands is a crucial ingredient in most of Camus's writings and a significant absence in the rest.

"The French of Algeria are a bastard race, made up of unexpected mixtures," wrote Camus in 1947. "Spaniards and Alsatians, Italians, Maltese Jews, and Greeks have met here. As in America, such intermingling has had happy results."[2] French Algeria's most renowned author was the descendant of, on his father's side, settlers from Bordeaux and, on his mother's, Spaniards from Minorca. Their intermingling did not result in an especially happy childhood for Albert Camus. Mobilized after the outbreak of World War I, the author's father, Lucien Auguste Camus, was mortally wounded at the First Battle of the Marne and died on 11 October 1914, barely eleven months after the birth of Albert. A father-son relationship is extremely rare in Camus's writings, and the one that is described, by Tarrou in autobiographical retrospect in *The Plague*, is very troubled.

Camus grew up in straitened circumstances in the proletarian Belcourt neighborhood of Algiers. Illiterate and partially deaf, his mother Catherine, who worked as a cleaning woman, would serve as the model for the silent, patient maternal figures who grace much of her son's writing. In *The Plague* she is the inspiration behind the mothers of both Rieux and Tarrou. As much as philosophical differences, Camus's background not only as an Algerian but as a child of poverty was responsible for the tensions that developed between him and the Parisian existentialists whose origins were primarily upper middle class. Camus's lifelong sympathy for the victim, similar to Tarrou's, can be traced to his own experiences at the bottom of the social hierarchy.

Camus did not attend any of the elite lycées that prepared others of his generation to be the cultural, political, and financial leaders of France. As a student at a local public school, however, he was befriended by teachers who recognized his talent and encouraged him to continue his education with scholarship support. He developed a passion for philosophy and wrote the thesis for his *diplôme d'études supérieures* on Neoplatonism and Christian theology, with particular emphasis on two figures also from North Africa: Plotinus and Augustine. He was to become a *philosophe* in the distinctively French tradition of moralists who, like Montaigne, Voltaire, Hugo, Zola, and Sartre, felt compelled to do more than hone their verbal craft, to act upon their convictions.

Camus would surely have become a philosophy teacher were it not for his affliction with tuberculosis, a disease that barred him from employment in a state-run school. Camus's first attack of tuberculosis occurred when he was 17, and bouts with the disease were to recur throughout his life—intimations of mortality for a man more preoccupied than most with the imminence of death. Throughout the first half of the twentieth century, tuberculosis was a pervasive and lethal disease for which there was no cure. Painful injections offered merely the hope of limited relief. It is understandable that, like his Oranians in *The Plague*, Camus felt for most of his life as if sentenced to death. For long periods of time, Camus was barred by disease from participating in his favorite physical activities, such as swimming and soccer. He was also exempted from military service and was even turned away when, at the outbreak of World War II, he attempted to enlist. Tuberculosis was a powerful inducement to concentrate the mind on matters of life and death and to alienate its victim from the ordinary routines of human existence. It is no exaggeration to claim that infirmity made Camus a writer, one acutely aware of the frail dominion of health. Part of Camus's success in making readers of his second novel feel that we all suffer from the plague derives from his ability to universalize his own ordeal with TB.

Much of Camus's earliest writing was journalistic. In 1937 he began working for the newly founded leftist newspaper *Alger-Républicain*, where, in a wide variety of roles and in covering a wide range of stories, he reinforced the commitment to clarity and veracity that would obsess Bernard Rieux while chronicling the Oran plague. Camus was a crusading journalist, intent on exposing injustice and oppression, particularly as products of the French colonialist system. In 1939 Camus traveled to Algeria's Kabylia region for a series of articles on poverty among its Arabs that anticipated what his fictional journalist Rambert's reports on the Arabs of Oran might have been like if the onset of plague had not cut short his mission.

The Author and His Work

After the demise of the *Alger-Républicain*, Camus worked for several months in France for *Paris-Soir*, a paper he despised because of its lack of political commitment. When a reduction in staff led to his dismissal in late 1940, Camus and his new, second wife, Francine Faure, moved in with her mother in her native town of Oran. Camus was struck by the contrast between lively Algiers and this drab, provincial second city of Algeria, which he berated as "the Chicago of our absurd Europe."[3] He was stuck in Oran for more than a year with little employment except sporadic work as a publisher's reader and as a private tutor to Jewish students restricted in matriculation by racist Vichy laws. It was during this time that he began work on a book about people caught in Oran for a bit less than a year after the arrival of the plague. The evolution of *The Plague* can be traced through Camus's notebooks and manuscripts until its publication seven years later, in 1947. He was almost as deliberate in his visions and revisions as his obsessive fictional author Joseph Grand.

When, in August 1942, a recurrence of tuberculosis became particularly severe, Camus, accompanied by Francine, sought relief in the mountain air of Le Panelier, a village in France's Massif Central where her cousin ran a boardinghouse. In the expectation that Camus would rejoin her soon, when he recovered, Francine returned to Oran for the opening of the term at the school where she taught mathematics. Before he could return to Oran, however, Allied forces entered North Africa, and the Germans, who had invaded France in 1940, extended their control of the country into the "free zone" that was administered by Marshal Henri Philippe Pétain's collaborationist regime based in Vichy. It became impossible to travel from Le Panelier to Oran, and Camus, like all the lovers separated by quarantine after the rats begin dying in *The Plague*, found himself cut off from his wife for the duration of the war. "Caught like rats!" is the phrase that Camus used in his journal entry for 11 November 1942 to describe the way he felt trapped.[4] Camus did most of the writing on his novel of privation while himself experiencing enforced solitude and exile from the people and landscapes he loved. Many of the names in *The Plague* are derived from those of people who lived in the vicinity of his exile. Though a Jesuit priest named Pain, whom Camus knew in Oran, might also be a source, Paneloux is thought by Jean Grenier to have borrowed his name from the town of Le Panelier.[5] The name Rieux echoes that of a local physician named Rioux, and Grand was the name of a neighbor, a farmer with whom Camus tried to grow tobacco.

Though he was honored with the Medal of the Liberation, and though by 1945 he was recognized as the principal intellectual spokesman of the French Resistance, Camus came late to anti-Nazi activities. Ill and ill at ease in chilly rural France, Camus, for all his leftist sympathies, hesitated for a long time before becoming involved in the organized political underground. He was apparently even oblivious to the anti-Nazi network of the clandestine newspaper *Combat* operating within the very neighborhood of Le Panelier. By 1944, however, after moving to Paris to work for the Gallimard publishing house, Camus had become the editor of *Combat*, himself writing hundreds of articles in opposition to the fascist oppressors and envisioning a new European order following their defeat. He credited the execution of the Communist leader Gabriel Péri with crystallizing his own commitment to resisting injustice and joining others in overthrowing tyranny. *Combat* monopolized a large part of Camus's abundant energies until 1945, when he resigned as its editor in order to complete work on *The Plague*.

The evolution of *The Plague*, during the course of which a central character, a lycée teacher named Stephan, was eliminated and Grand and Rambert were added, can be traced through the *Notebooks* (1963, 1965) and *Les Archives de "La Peste,"* the discarded fragments of the novel that Camus published in *Les Cahiers de la Pléiade* in April 1947. The long gestation of *The Plague*, while its author was lonely, isolated, and idle and then energized by the urgency of a common cause into a prolific output of journalism, philosophy, drama, and fiction, accounts for some of the difficulties in pinning down the novel's allegorical intentions. Perhaps because Camus's own ideas were evolving, critics have puzzled over whether the Oran epidemic should be read as an internal or external challenge and whether the enemy is abstract or concrete. The fact that, at the beginning of the novel, Rieux scorns the indifference and passivity of his fellow citizens yet by the story's end affirms their innocence might be explained by Camus's own development during most of an extraordinary decade. These grim and exhilarating years were responsible for Camus's most remarkable philosophical statement, *The Myth of Sisyphus*, as well as his most influential theatrical works, including *The Misunderstanding* and *Caligula* (1945). Following *The Plague*, Camus produced, in collaboration with the actor and director Jean-Louis Barrault, the play *State of Siege*, which, though set in plague-afflicted Cadiz, Camus always insisted was not a theatrical adaptation of his novel.

Camus personally and the world in general experienced hardships and horrors during the years that *The Plague* was being plotted. This book's belabored birth in the turmoil and torment of the midtwentieth century lends some credence to the French adage *Nul bien sans peine*— There is no gain without pain. "Of course," wrote Camus in his diary while working on the novel, "we know that the plague has its good side, that it opens eyes, that it forces us to think."[6] So, too, with *The Plague*, and what precisely the novel compels us to think about is the burden of this book. *The Plague* remains a dramatic document of the crises peculiar to those who lived through the Occupation of France during the 1940s. It is history translated into fiction, and while an understanding of its specific coordinates of place and time is crucial to its appreciation, *The Plague* also demonstrates the ability of history and fiction to transcend themselves with truths of enduring significance.

14

Lessons of *The Plague*

O happy generation of our great-grandsons who will not have known
these miseries and perhaps will consider our testimony as fable!
—Petrarch, after more than half the population
of Florence perished in the Black Death.[1]

Set in an indeterminate year ("194_"), in an obscure city (Oran) that,
to Americans, might as well be Oz, *The Plague* was, before 1980,
easily read as a fable. Polio has been vanquished, and the smallpox
virus survives only in a few laboratories. Aside from periodic visita-
tions of influenza, usually more of a nuisance than a killer, epidemics,
at least until the outbreak of cholera in Peru in 1991, have been as
common in this hemisphere as flocks of auks. Those of us who first
read *The Plague* during the era of the Salk and Sabin vaccines were
hard put to imagine a distant world not yet domesticated by biotech-
nology, in which a mere bacillus could terrorize an entire city. We did
not read *The Plague* as the story of a plague, since the typhus outbreak
near Oran that caused the city to be quarantined in 1941 and resulted
in more than 75,000 deaths was only a source, not the novel's subject.
Pestilence seemed unlikely to menace our own modern cities. The
story was a pretext, an occasion for ethical speculation—in short, an
allegory. "It is not pure coincidence that Lucretius' poem ends with a
prodigious image of the sanctuaries of the gods swollen with the accus-
ing corpses of plague victims," wrote Camus of the Latin poem *De
Rerum natura (On the Nature of Things)*.[2] And it is surely no accident

that his own novel is shaped by the virulent epidemic in Oran. Nor is it impertinent to ask what is the thematic function of plague in *The Plague*.

Camus himself encouraged such speculation. It was the way he read Herman Melville's *Moby-Dick*, a novel he revered not merely as a story of the hunt for the great white whale but, somewhat like *The Plague* as well, as "one of the most overwhelming myths ever invented on the subject of the struggle of man against evil."[3] However, in a widely publicized letter sent to the critic Roland Barthes in 1955, Camus reacted against those who had alleged that in *The Plague* he evades historical realities. He insisted that his book be read not as a study in abstract evil but as a story whose manifest reference is to the situation of France under the Nazi occupation:

> *The Plague*, which I wanted to be read on a number of levels, nevertheless has as its obvious content the struggle of the European resistance movements against Nazism. The proof of this is that although the specific enemy is nowhere named, everyone in every European country recognized it. Let me add that a long extract from *The Plague* appeared during the Occupation, in a collection of underground texts, and that this fact alone would justify the transposition I made. In a sense, *The Plague* is more than a chronicle of the Resistance. But certainly it is nothing less.[4]

"Never trust the artist. Trust the tale" was D. H. Lawrence's advice about the remarks that authors often offer about their own work. Should Camus, who was at a personal and professional impasse a decade after writing what many regard as his masterwork, be trusted in his commentary on *The Plague*? In the notebooks he kept while writing *The Plague*, Camus also claims World War II, as well as the human condition, as the subtext to the story he was setting in Oran: "I want to express by means of the plague the stifling air from which we all suffered and the atmosphere of threat and exile in which we lived. I want at the same time to extend that interpretation to the notion of existence in general. The plague will give the image of those who in this war were lifted to reflection, to silence—and to moral anguish."[5] The privations of World War II and the resistance to oppression certainly provided the context during which Camus wrote his novel, and undeniable parallels exist between the hardships of Vichy France and those of quarantined Oran. The filmmaker Pierre Sauvage more recently reaffirmed the connection. *Weapons of the Spirit*—his 1988 documentary about Chambon-sur-Lignon, a largely Huguenot town in the mountains of the southern French department of Haute Loire that courageously sheltered 5,000 Jews, mostly children, after the German invasion—begins with an epigraph from *The Plague*. The cited quotation is one of several passages in the novel that proclaim the modest responsibility to attest that two plus two equals four. Later in the film, Sauvage comments on the similarity between the dedicated way that Camus's Oranians do what has to be done to combat the plague and the quiet dignity with which the people of Chambon, near the village of Le Panelier where Camus in fact spent part of the war, defied the Nazi genocide.

It should be noted that French sympathetic to the Resistance commonly referred to the Nazis as *la peste brune*—the brown plague. And the novel itself even makes explicit the analogy between plague and war. "There have been as many plagues as wars in history," announces Rieux shortly after allowing himself to recognize the onset of the epidemic in Oran, "yet always plagues and wars take people equally by surprise" (34). If the analogy rested merely on statistical frequency, however, he might as well have told a story about earthquakes. And if surprise is the chief criterion for comparison to war, Harold Pinter's *The Birthday Party* (1958) might have served as well.

There are important differences between life in wartime France and the experience in *The Plague*, not least being the fact that the Nazi occupation was a human tyranny whereas the Oran epidemic is a natural calamity. The invasions, persecutions, and exterminations that plagued Europe during the 1940s were a result of human choice and human agency and could be resisted by human actions. By contrast, Camus's plague is a phenomenon that defies motivation, comprehension, or opposition. Metaphysical questions are not always interchangeable with social ones. Our ethical responsibilities in responding to despotism or disease are different.

However, even if they were not, even if we imagined that Nazism were as incurable as the mysterious malady that devastates the population of Oran, *The Plague* as an allegory of the Occupation would be reduced to a document of antiquarian interest. Decades after the Allied victory, the political and social organization of Europe and the rest of the world is vastly changed from 194_, and *The Plague* would not continue to be so compelling to so many if it were merely a disguised account of the struggle against Hitler. In fact, if merely that, it would be reasonable to ask: Why disguise the account? Why not, in the spirit of the plain-talking Tarrou, dispense altogether with the coyness of allegory and tell the story that you want to tell?

Perhaps the book *is* about a plague. But then why should healthy readers be disturbed by a medical oddity in distant Oran? *The Plague* assumed a greater urgency during the 1980s, when it became apparent that plagues were not obsolete occurrences or quaint events confined to distant regions. At a 1982 Washington, D.C., meeting, leading scientists, public health officials, and gay rights activists coined the acronym AIDS to refer to the acquired immune deficiency syndrome that had—even before a 1981 article in the *New England Journal of Medicine* reporting on seven inexplicable cases of severe infection— begun to spread throughout the world. By the end of the decade, AIDS was a global epidemic, and millions were HIV-positive—afflicted with the precondition of AIDS, human immunodeficiency virus. At first, AIDS seemed to target homosexual men and intravenous drug users, but like Camus's plague, it was soon striking capriciously, without any regard to the social status of its hundreds of thousands of helpless victims. As in *The Plague*, a panicked populace responded in a variety of ways, and no cure was found.

Published in 1987, *And the Band Played on: Politics, People, and the AIDS Epidemic* is a detailed account of the spread of AIDS and of the spectrum of reactions to it. What, to a student of Camus, is remarkable about Randy Shilts's book—which was a best-seller in both hardcover and paperback—is how much it has in common with *The Plague*. Not only does Shilts document the same pattern of initial denial followed by acknowledgment, recrimination, terror, and occasional stoical heroism that Rieux recounts during the Oran ordeal. But it is clear that Shilts has read Camus and has adopted much of the style and structure of *The Plague* to tell his story of an actual plague. Of the nine sections to *And the Band Played on*, four of them—parts 4, 5, 6, and 7—begin with a different epigraph from Camus's novel. In part 2, describing baffling new developments among homosexual patients, Shilts echoes Camus's absurdist *Myth of Sisyphus* when he states: "The fight against venereal diseases was proving a Sisyphean task."[6] Like Rieux, who personifies his plague as an enemy aroused from sleep, Shilts explains that, by the end of 1980, "slowly and almost imperceptibly, the killer was awakening."[7] In the final line of his chronicle, Camus's Rieux reminds us that any victory over plague is only provisional, "that the plague bacillus never dies or disappears for good; that it can lie dormant for years and years in furniture and linen-chests; that it bides its time in bedrooms, cellars, trunks, and bookshelves; and that perhaps the day would come when, for the bane and the enlightening of men, it would rouse up its rats again and send them forth to die in a happy city" (278). Shilts's view of human arrogance toward natural adversity seems shaped not only by his research into the often cavalier or inept responses to AIDS but also by his reading of *The Plague*. His account, for example, of *Pneumocystis* pneumonia, a disease that frequently results from a failure of immune systems, sounds remarkably like the final sentence of the Camus novel. Like Rieux, Shilts provides an admonition against overconfidence, since the disease will never be definitively defeated: "*Pneumocystis* flared sporadically, eager to take advantage of any opportunity to thrive in its preferred ecological niche, the lung. The disease, however, would disappear simultaneously once the immune system was restored. And the little creature would return to an obscure place in medical books where it was recorded as one of the thousands of microorganisms that always lurk on the fringes of human existence, lying dormant until infrequent opportunity allows it to burst forth and follow the biological dictate to grow and multiply."[8]

Camus's culminating vision of horror temporarily abated but eternally dormant is also appropriated by another American author, to conclude his study of the contagion of repression that afflicted Hollywood. Stefan Kanfer borrows the title of his 1973 book, *A Journal of the Plague Years*, from the Defoe novel, but its spirit is indebted more to Camus.[9] Kanfer begins his chronicle of the rise and fall of blacklists in American movie studios with an epigraph from *The Plague*. The attempt by the House Un-American Activities Committee (HUAC) and private vigilante groups to purge the movie industry of anyone suspected of leftist sympathies was most successful during the years immediately after the publication of *The Plague*. In retrospect, Kanfer, stretching Camus's novel into a political allegory extending beyond Oran, warns that the eventual disbanding of HUAC and the end of blacklisting a few years after Camus's death, represent only a provisional victory over the forces of ideological reaction. Complacency and compliancy encourage their return. *A Journal of the Plague Years* gives its final words, as it gave its opening ones, to Camus, and they are the final words of *The Plague*, the admonition that the plague is always lurking, biding its time to send forth its rats to die again.

Rieux's diagnosis of his fellow townspeople is uncertain and his prognosis wary; he is aware that plague bacilli never vanish but merely bide their time for an inevitable resurgence. The etiology of the epidemic that strikes Oran remains unclear. Its emergence in Oran in 194_, like its choice of victims, seems gratuitous and capricious. Furthermore, baffled by the randomness of its ravages, neither Rieux nor any of his medical colleagues can offer an effective Rx. Nevertheless, both Rieux and Camus submit their account of the experience of Oran under the plague as a lesson to the rest of us. The plague and *The Plague* are presumed to be didactic, but exactly how and what they teach remain problematic. In the final pages, Rieux's asthmatic patient poses what is in effect the epic question for the entire book. The old man talks about the pride Oranians have begun to feel in having survived the plague. "But what does that mean—'plague'?" he asks, as if he were a student trying to decode Camus's allegory. His own reply, "Just life, no more than that" (277), begs the question by suggesting another, even more elusive one: What is life? If *The Plague* could answer that question, it would be a sacred text. The fact that it implicitly raises the ultimate question makes Camus's book at least a haunted one.

Despite momentary jubilation over the disappearance of the plague, Rieux concludes his chronicle with a warning that "perhaps the day would come when, *for the bane and the enlightening of men* [italics mine], it would rouse up its rats again and send them forth to die in a happy city." What sort of enlightenment do the plague and *The Plague* provide? It is likely that Camus chose Daniel Defoe as the source for the epigraph to his own book in part because the English author—whom Camus calls Daniel De Foe—also wrote an important plague narrative, *A Journal of the Plague Year*. In his 1722 novel, Defoe likewise recounts the collective story of one city, London, under the impact of a plague and uses a narrator so self-effacing that his only concession to personal identity is the placement of his initials, H.F., at the very end. But the particular passage cited in *The Plague*'s epigraph, which comes from the preface to volume 3 of *Robinson Crusoe*, immediately raises questions of representation: "It is as reasonable to represent one kind of imprisonment by another, as it is to represent anything that really exists by that which exists not." Coming before the reader has even met the first infected rat in Oran, the Defoe passage is an invitation to allegory, a signal that the fiction that follows signifies more than the story of a town in Algeria. In an early stage of composition, Camus noted that he did not want to call his book *The Plague* but rather something like *The Prisoners*, perhaps to highlight its theme of universal incarceration, the sense that, as represented by Oran, all the world's a dungeon.[10]

Camus's 1955 letter to Roland Barthes interpreted *The Plague*, of course, as an oblique commentary on the bleak ordeal of Nazi tyranny. And it is clear, from his notebooks and from the resentment of some of his comrades on the left, that by the time he finished writing *The Plague*, Camus was also experiencing and expressing increasing anxiety over Communist oppression. Plagues are natural phenomena, however, whereas the arrest, torture, and execution of innocent people are acts of human agency, for which talk of accountability, prevention, control, and retribution makes much more sense. Both pestilence and dictatorship—by the likes of Hitler or Stalin—must be resisted, but it is much easier and more sensible for Tarrou to refuse judgment on a bacillus than on the Gestapo. It is courageous and correct for Rieux, Tarrou, Grand, and the others to oppose a disease with uncompromising stubbornness, but it is questionable whether they would adopt the same strategy if the enemy were human brutes who had already made good on their pledge to retaliate, with the slaughter of innocent hostages, for any act of sabotage. The plague-fighting Tarrou appears admirable in his opposition to any killing whatsoever, but it is not clear how he would fight a human plague like fascism. Sanitary squads would be ineffective against Auschwitz. Some such groups in fact helped choose which Jews to send to the death camps.

Though allegories were commonplace in the Middle Ages, when art was expected to be didactic, even doctrinal, they became unfashionable in the modern period, which proclaimed the independence of the artist from the obligation to teach or even represent anything. Art is for the sake of art, proclaimed artists at the turn of the century, not for the sake of making a statement. "A poem should not mean / But be," declares Archibald MacLeish in his 1926 poem "Ars Poetica," and means it.[11] In his 1850 essay "The Poetic Principle," Edgar Allan Poe was already denouncing what he called "the heresy of the didactic."[12] His eminent translator, Charles Baudelaire, also insisted that literature have no pedagogical agenda. In 1861, scorning what he called "the heresy of didacticism with its inevitable corollaries, the heresies of passion, truth, and morality," Baudelaire explained: "Most people assume that the object of poetry is some kind of teaching, that it must now fortify conscience, now perfect manners, now, in sum, demonstrate something useful. Poetry, however little one descends into oneself, interrogates one's soul, recalls one's memories of enthusiasm, has no object but itself: it can have no other, and no poem will be so great, so noble, so truly worthy of the name of poem as that which has been written solely for the pleasure of writing a poem."[13] To the commonplace notion that literature offers moral instruction, Oscar Wilde, who also fought the "didactic heresy," countered, in his 1891 preface to *The Picture of Dorian Gray*: "There is no such thing as a moral or an immoral book. Books are well written, or badly written. That is all."[14] All that movies do, claimed producers, is tell a story.

"If you want to send a message," insisted Hollywood mogul Samuel Goldwyn, "Go see Western Union."[15] Western literature of the twentieth century has been uncomfortable with the role of messenger. It prefers showing over telling, reporting over editorializing. Like Rieux, it finds something dishonest in commentary.

Yet Rieux's text is not merely a chronicle, and Camus is not often thought of as a writer indifferent to passion, truth, and morality. In a sense, *The Plague* is a rather old-fashioned attempt to pursue philosophy through images. The image of a populace tormented by ganglia, fever, and convulsions is evoked not for its own sake but for the ideas of human suffering it elicits. However, the novel is certainly more than an easy adage; Paneloux's sermons are not the paradigm for Camus's achievement. If *The Plague* could be summarized in a few moral maxims, there would, of course, have been no reason to write or read almost 300 pages.

Many of the earliest reviews of *The Plague* established the continuing terms of debate over whether the book's philosophical ambitions undercut its aesthetic achievement. Writing in the *Yale Review*, Orville Prescott, for example, faulted the work for using fiction merely as a vehicle for abstract ideas: "M. Camus is a clear thinker and effective writer. There is evidence in this book that he could be a fine novelist if he cared to. . . . But instead of writing about particular people he has written about people who are abstract symbols of various political and moral attitudes, never interesting human beings."[16] On the front page of the *New York Times Book Review*, Stephen Spender defended the book *despite* what he saw as its message-mongering:

> *The Plague* is parable and sermon, and should be considered as such. To criticize it by standards which apply to most fiction would be to risk condemning it for moralizing, which is exactly where it is strongest. *The Plague* stands or falls by its message. The message is not the highest form of creative art, but it may be of such importance for our time that to dismiss it in the name of artistic criticism would be to blaspheme against the human spirit. What we have to judge is the urgency, for us, of M. Camus' morality. It seems to me to be of so much urgency that we would be wrong to ask how much significance people may attach to it tomorrow.[17]

Tomorrow and tomorrow and tomorrow have crept on, and people throughout the world have continued to attach urgent importance to the novel. Perhaps that is because, as Milton Rugoff contended on the same day Spender's review appeared: "*The Plague* is not a tract in disguise or an object lesson enlivened by colored slides. It is an extraordinarily vivid account of a city of men living as intensely and self-consciously as men can live. . . . Because *The Plague* is a novel of man as a member of a group rather than as an individual intent on a private career, it is an unfamiliar literary tradition. But it will, I think, become a marker on the landscape of contemporary fiction."[18]

Camus learned the lesson of more than a century of aesthetic suspicion toward lessons. Discussing the responsibilities of fiction, in *The Myth of Sisyphus*, he distinguishes between philosophical writing—which is provisional, suggestive, and open—and thesis-mongering, which is absolutist and constrictive. "The great novelists," he insists, "are philosophical novelists—that is, the contrary of thesis-writers. For instance, Balzac, Sade, Melville, Stendhal, Dostoevsky, Proust, Malraux, Kafka, to cite but a few."[19] For Camus, great writers, by immersing us in history and particularity, free us to imagine human possibilities. They do not reject the concrete, the specific, and the contingent in pursuit of the abstract, the general, and the eternal: "The essential is that the novelists should triumph in the concrete and that this constitute their nobility. This wholly carnal triumph has been prepared for them by a thought in which abstract powers have been humiliated."[20]

It is significant that the epidemic in Oran is frequently referred to in *The Plague* as "*l'abstraction*." As with all other French nouns preceded by a definite article, the term is ambiguous. It could refer either to a particular phenomenon or to a universal, the abstraction or abstraction. *Le pain*, for example, could be translated as "the bread," that is, the particular loaf of pumpernickel that sat on your dinner table Tuesday night. Or else it could be rendered as the general concept "bread," as used in a discourse on the importance of bread and circuses to human happiness. *L'abstraction* is both "the abstraction" and "abstraction" in general, though an English translator is forced to choose between the two.

As *the* abstraction, the specific plague that afflicts the people of Oran in 194_ is a distraction from their customary activities and a diversion of their energies. "Yes, he'd make a fresh start, once the period of 'abstractions' was over" (253), Rieux assures himself, conceiving of the disease as a temporary detour from ordinary life. He is, of course, mistaken, as only a few pages later he receives the telegram that informs him that his wife is dead. There will never be a fresh start to the Rieux marriage, and for the chronicler at least, "the period of abstractions" will never be entirely over. Nor can it in fact be over for any of us if we take seriously Tarrou's portentous comments that he was infected with plague long before coming to Oran and that indeed everyone is infected with the disease:

> I know positively—yes, Rieux, I can say I know the world inside out, as you may see—that each of us has the plague within him; no one, no one on earth is free from it. And I know, too, that we must keep endless watch on ourselves lest in a careless moment we breathe in somebody's face and fasten the infection on him. What's natural is the microbe. All the rest—health, integrity, purity (if you like)— is a product of the human will, of a vigilance that must never falter. The good man, the man who infects hardly anyone, is the man who has the fewest lapses of attention. (229)

Such sententious rhetoric transforms the disease that abstracts Oran into an abstraction, a symbol that comes perilously close to expressing a thesis. The abstraction that torments Rieux, Tarrou, Rambert, and the others ceases to be a particular historical phenomenon and is recruited to illustrate an enduring truth about the human condition. Susan Sontag, for one, has argued strenuously against appropriating a disease as a figure of speech to explain other phenomena, as well as against appropriating figures of speech to explain a disease. In *Illness as Metaphor* (1978), she examines how tuberculosis and cancer especially have been conceived figuratively, thereby adding an intellectual disfigurement to the physical damage done to their victims; it is horrible enough to suffer from a malignant tumor without being conceptualized as a fortress under siege. And when used as tropes for other topics, such fanciful images in turn compromise our ability to think lucidly about them, as when, for example, we talk about a cancer that is attacking the body politic. "My point," declares Sontag pointedly, "is that illness is *not* a metaphor, and that the most truthful way of regarding illness—and the healthiest way of being ill—is one most purified of, most resistant to, metaphoric thinking."[21] Yet she also acknowledges that, since all language is metaphorical, it is impossible to avoid any figure of speech in a discussion of disease. Being aware, however, of our inevitable impulse toward abstraction can help to free us from it. "It is toward an elucidation of those metaphors, and a liberation from them, that I dedicate this inquiry," says Sontag about her book *Illness as Metaphor.*[22]

Camus is similarly vigilant about the abstractions of rhetoric, the way in which language distracts us from concentrating on the immediate truth that two plus two equals four. Much of *The Rebel* is a polemic against abstraction, the human temptation toward the inhuman, toward conceptual systems that ignore the messy details of particular people in specific times and places. Armed with such abstractions, we can conscientiously march off to murder. It is easier to slaughter individual human beings if we treat them as abstractions and fortify ourselves with absolute doctrines. Airy precepts of Aryan supremacy as well as the act of stripping, shearing, and numbering millions of individuals enabled the Nazi death camp administrators to distance themselves from the savage immediacy of mass slaughter. After the war, many of the Nazi leaders who stood trial for war crimes in Nuremburg offered as their defense the excuse that "they were just following orders," as though the chain of command insulated them from personal responsibility for atrocity and the abstraction of duty superseded the sufferings of particular human beings.

What impelled the adolescent Jean Tarrou to run away from home was the abstractedness of his righteous father. For his hobby, Tarrou *père* delighted in memorizing the intricacies of railway routes, as if they were a mathematical puzzle disconnected from any actual geographical locales. In his account to Rieux of the experience of attending a capital criminal trial, Tarrou *fils* recalls being shocked by the manner in which his prosecutor father was able to demand a human being's execution by treating him as an abstraction: "the defendant." Prior to his first visit to a courtroom, "[m]y notions on the subject were purely abstract," he explains, "and I'd never given it serious thought" (224). What he can never cease thinking seriously about is his discovery that the neat abstractions of the criminal justice system masked the human reality of a living individual, in this particular case a man with the particular traits of sparse, sandy hair, an untidy tie, and the habit of biting the nails on only his right hand. The man was probably guilty, but Tarrou rebels against the facile device of reducing a human being to a mere defendant, a disembodied abstraction that much easier to behead with the guillotine.

Camus distinguishes between revolution and rebellion in favor of the latter:

> The mystification peculiar to the mind which claims to be revolutionary today sums up and increases bourgeois mystification. It contrives, by the promise of absolute justice, the acceptance of perpetual injustice, of unlimited compromise, and of indignity. Rebellion itself only aspires to the relative and can only promise an assured dignity coupled with relative justice. It supposes a limit at which the community of man is established. Its universe is the universe of relative values.[23]

His aversion to revolutionary abstractions led Camus to oppose totalitarian systems, like fascism and communism, that arrogantly substitute a formula of human experience for the experience itself. He recognized that the Nazis and their collaborationist killers were no different in kind from those who appealed to abstract doctrines to justify the orgy of violent retribution that immediately followed the Liberation in 1945. Antipathy to abstractions earned Camus the pejorative label of "moderate" and the enmity of ideologues during the political polarization of the 1960s and 1970s. In fighting the faceless slayer of Oran, Tarrou is in effect resisting facelessness, taking a stand against abstraction. Perhaps that is part of what Camus meant by his comment to Barthes that *The Plague* has as its content the struggle of the European

Resistance against Nazism. If the book is indeed an allegory, it is in a sense an allegory against allegorization. Nazism, Stalinism, and other totalitarianisms offer comprehensive allegories to explain (away) all of history.

"*The Plague* shows that the absurd *teaches nothing*," wrote Camus in his notebook, perhaps in a moment of despair.²⁴ But to say that, as evidenced by *The Plague*, the absurd teaches nothing is not the same as to claim that *The Plague* teaches nothing. Nor is teaching nothing identical with not teaching. "I want something which is just," wrote Camus elsewhere in his notebooks, and then replied: "That is exactly what the plague is."²⁵ Just how the plague can be that is not amenable to easy interpretation. Camus's novel provides a valuable lesson in the inadequacy of lessons, in the presumptuousness of imposing a single, imperial system on the chaos of existence. Perhaps that is also what Camus means by the cryptic phrase in his notebook: "*The liberating plague*."²⁶ The plague that forces an onerous quarantine on the people of Oran is not manifestly liberating, except to the extent that it frees victims and readers to reexamine fundamental questions. Anyone who has been through the plague or *The Plague* is no longer enslaved to narrow views of life and death. Though he insists on an attitude of revolt, Camus recognizes the redeeming value of evil, that "the plague has its good side, that it opens eyes, that it forces us to think. In this regard it is like all the evils of this world and the world itself."²⁷

Disappointed that Rieux is unwilling to help him escape from Oran and return to his lover in Paris, Rambert scolds the doctor: "You can't understand. You're using the language of reason, not of the heart; you live in a world of abstractions" (79). The lesson that Rieux learns through the microbial abstraction that terrorizes his town for the rest of the year is one about the peril of abstractions. By throwing himself into the abstraction of the actual plague, Rieux ceases to live in a world of abstractions. The way to fight disease is through inoculation with the malady itself. Reflecting on the accusation of heartless abstraction that Rambert has flung at him, Rieux reflects: "Yes, an element of abstraction, of a divorce from reality, entered into such calamities. Still when abstraction sets to killing you, you've got to get busy with it" (81). You've got to fight abstraction with abstraction. When he returns to the ordeal as its chronicler, Rieux has become aware that the enlightenment that the plague bacillus returns to provide is limited and provisional. Antitotalitarian, it is a lesson in the limits of enlightenment and the dangers of abstraction.

The book's title, *La Peste*, conveys the same ambiguity as *l'abstraction*. "The plague" is an obvious reference to the fictionalized experience of the people of Oran from April to February of a year in the 1940s when Tarrou, Grand, Paneloux, and others contend with and contract the disease. But the novel is also about "plague," a general concept that transcends the particulars of a North African port during the middle of the twentieth century. The most intriguing and confounding paradox of Camus's book is that it so manifestly uses plague for abstract meditations on the hazards of abstraction. That is a point missed by many of Camus's detractors, who fault *The Plague* for its own abstractness. The Hungarian Marxist George Lukacs, for one, noted Camus's failure to create rounded characters: "For, however suggestive as an allegory of the *condition humaine*, and however subtle the moral problems brought up by Camus's description of the plague, the characters in *La Peste* remain, by Camus's definition, shadows."[28] An American critic, Donald Lazere, likewise expresses disappointment: "After the first reading, without the suspense and emotional involvement in the characters' fates, Rieux, Tarrou, Cottard, and Paneloux do not retain enough individual complexity or appeal to become much more than the abstract voices of philosophical positions."[29] It is up to the individual reader to determine whether the novel's deliberate denial of individual complexity in order to demonstrate the importance of individual complexity is a flaw or a strength.

As though the plague were a pretext for character analysis and *The Plague* a text to announce the results, each of Camus's characters is tested by the ordeal. Though everyone in one way or another is afflicted with plague, and some die from it, all, with the exception of Cottard, receive a bill of health. On the basis of his own direct observations and the information he has scrupulously acquired from others, Rieux, on the final page of his report, can thus honestly "state quite simply what we learn in a time of pestilence: that there are more things to admire in men than to despise" (278). It is a sentimental and abstract conclusion, but one that is supported by the evidence that Camus has contrived for Rieux to examine. Readers need not subscribe to Rieux's modest affirmation of human benevolence to conclude that there are many more things in *The Plague* to admire than to despise.

NOTES AND REFERENCES

Chapter 1

1. Robert Greer Cohn, "The True Camus," *French Review* 60, no. 1 (October 1986): 38.

Chapter 2

1. Albert Camus, review of *Nausea, Alger-républicain*, 12 March 1939, in *Lyrical and Critical Essays*, ed. Philip Thody, trans. Ellen Conroy Kennedy (New York: Vintage, 1970), 199.

2. Catherine E. Campbell, "A Survey of Graduate Reading Lists in French," *French Review* 56 (March 1983): 588–96.

3. Gaëtan Picon, "Notes on *The Plague*," trans. Ellen Conroy Kennedy, in *Camus: A Collection of Critical Essays*, ed. Germaine Brée (Englewood Cliffs, N.J.: Prentice-Hall, 1962), 145.

4. Germaine Brée, *Camus*, rev. ed.(New York: Harcourt, Brace & World, 1964), 130.

Chapter 3

1. See André Abbou, "La Deuxième Vie d'Albert Camus: Paradoxes d'une singulière aventure de notre culture" in (Albert Camus's Second Life: Paradoxes of a Single Adventure in Our Culture) *Albert Camus 1980*, Raymond Gay-Crosier, ed. (Gainesville: University Presses of Florida, 1980), 277–88.

2. Quoted in Philip Thody, *Albert Camus, 1913–1960* (New York: Macmillan, 1962), 107.

3. Jean-Paul Sartre, *What Is Literature?* trans. Bernard Frechtman (New York: Harper & Row, 1965), 290.

4. Jean-Paul Sartre, "Albert Camus," in *Situations*, trans. Benita Eisler (New York: George Braziller, 1965), 110.

5. Jean Pouillon, "L'Optimisme de Camus" (The Optimism of Camus), *Les Temps modernes* 26 (November 1947): 926.

6. Jean Catesson, "A propos de *La Peste*" (Concerning *The Plague*) *Cahiers du sud* 287 (1948): 144–49.

7. René Etiemble, "Peste ou peché?" (Plague or Sin?) *Les Temps modernes* 26 (November 1947): 911–20.

8. Justin O'Brien, review of *The Plague*, *New Republic* (16 August 1948): 23.

9. Robert Kee, review of *The Plague*, *Spectator* (3 September 1948): 314.

10. Quoted in Herbert R. Lottman, *Albert Camus: A Biography* (Garden City, N.Y.: Doubleday, 1979), 601.

11. Susan Sontag, *Against Interpretation* (New York: Farrar, Straus & Giroux, 1966), 53.

12. J. J. Brochier, *Albert Camus: Philosophe pour classes terminales* (Albert Camus: Philosopher for Terminal Classes) (Paris: Balland, 1970), quoted in Patrick McCarthy, *Camus* (New York: Random House, 1982), 327.

13. Thody, Camus, 106.

14. See Emily Tall, "Camus in the Soviet Union: Some Recent Emigrés Speak," *Comparative Literature Studies* 16 (September 1979): 237–49.

15. Albert Camus, *Notebooks 1942–1951*, tr. Justin O'Brien (New York: Knopf, 1965), 135.

16. Claudine and Jacques Broyelle, *Le Bonheur des Pierres* (The Happiness of Stones) (Paris: Seuil, 1978), 49, quoted in McCarthy, *Camus*, 327.

17. Albert Camus, review of *On a Philosophy of Expression* by Brice Parain, in *Lyrical and Critical Essays*, 240.

18. Serge Doubrovsky, "Camus in America," in Brée, *Camus*, 17.

19. Letter to author from Random House editor Anne Freedgood, 31 August 1981.

20. Sontag, *Against Interpretation*, 55.

21. Jack Newfield, *Robert Kennedy: A Memoir* (New York: E. P. Dutton, 1969), 58–59.

22. Robert Penn Warren, *Who Speaks for the Negro?* (New York: Random House, 1965), 95, quoted in Donald Lazere, *The Unique Creation of Albert Camus*, (New Haven: Yale University Press, 1973), 244–45.

23. William Styron, *Darkness Visible: A Memoir of Madness*. (New York: Random House, 1990), 21–22.

24. Athol Fugard, *Notebooks 1960–1977*, ed. Mary Benson (London: Faber and Faber, 1983), 94.

Notes and References

Chapter 4

1. James Joyce, *A Portrait of the Artist as a Young Man* (New York: Viking, 1956), 215.

2. Fyodor Dostoyevski, *The Devils*, trans. David Magarshack (Baltimore: Penguin, 1971), 21.

3. Interview with Albert Camus, *Paru*, no. 47 (1948): 7–13, translated and quoted in Philip Thody, *Albert Camus: A Study of His Work* (New York: Grove, 1957), 38.

4. Albert Camus, "The Artist at Work," in *Exile and the Kingdom*, trans. Justin O'Brien (New York: Vintage, 1958), 158.

5. Albert Camus, letter to Roland Barthes, 11 January 1955, in *Lyrical and Critical Essays*, 339.

6. Albert Camus, *The Rebel: An Essay on Man in Revolt*, trans. Anthony Bower (New York: Knopf, 1971), 22.

7. *Notebooks 1942–1951*, 137.

8. Albert Camus, "Discours de Suède," in *Essais*, ed. Roger Quilliot and L. Faucon (Paris: Gallimard, Bibliothèque de la Pléiade, 1965), 1071–72. (translation mine).

Chapter 5

1. George Orwell, "Why I Write" (1947), in *A Collection of Essays* (Garden City, N.Y.: Doubleday/Anchor, 1954), 320.

2. *Notebooks 1942–1951*, 40.

3. Albert Camus, *The Myth of Sisyphus and Other Essays*, trans. Justin O'Brien (New York: Knopf, 1955), 120.

4. Ibid., 121.

5. Ibid., 123.

6. Ibid., 11.

7. Translation mine.

8. Albert Camus, "Discours du 10 décembre 1957," in *Essais*, 1073 (Translation mine).

9. Albert Camus, *Notebooks 1935–1942*, tr. Philip Thody (New York: Knopf, 1963), 143.

Chapter 7

1. Ernest Hemingway, *A Moveable Feast* (New York: Bantam, 1965), 12.

2. *Notebooks 1942–1951*, 136.

3. Ibid, 137.

Chapter 8

1. Albert Camus, "Intelligence and the Scaffold," *Lyrical and Critical Essays*, 211.

2. Ibid., 212.

3. Roland Barthes, *Writing Degree Zero and Elements of Semiology*, trans. Annette Lavers and Colin Smith (Boston: Beacon, 1970), 76.

4. Ibid., 77.

5. Brian T. Fitch, *The Narcissistic Text: A Reading of Camus' Fiction* (Toronto: University of Toronto Press; 1982), 15.

6. Albert Camus, *L'Homme révolté* (The Rebel), in *Essais*, 664 (translation mine). In his translation of *The Rebel*, Anthony Bower misleadingly translates this as: "Romantic activities undoubtedly imply a rejection of reality" (260).

7. Alain Robbe-Grillet, "Nature, Humanism, Tragedy," *For a New Novel: Essays on Fiction*, trans. Richard Howard (New York: Grove, 1965), 64.

8. Robbe-Grillet, "A Future for the Novel," in *For a New Novel*, 19.

9. Translation and italics mine. Stuart Gilbert translates this, misleadingly, as: "an unusual type of chronicle, since the writer seems to make a point of understatement" (22).

10. Oeuvres Sociales de la Mutuelle Générale de la Sûreté, National d'Oran, *Guide de la ville d'Oran* (Imprimérie de la Lyre, n.d.), 220–21, translated and quoted in Martha O'Nan, "Biographical Context and Its Importance to Classroom Study," in *Approaches to Teaching Camus's "The Plague,"* ed. Steven G. Kellman (New York: Modern Language Association, 1985), 106.

11. *Notebooks 1935–1942*, 187.

12. Albert Camus, "The Minotaur, or, Stopping in Oran," in *Lyrical and Critical Essays*, 116.

13. Ibid., 113.

14. Ibid., 116.

15. Richard McLaughlin, review of *The Plague*, *Saturday Review of Literature* (31 July 1948): 10.

16. *Lyrical and Critical Essays*, 109.

17. Quoted in O'Nan, "Biographical Context," 103.

18. Camus, "The Minotaur," in *Lyrical and Critical Essays*, 116.

19. Albert Camus, preface to "The Wrong Side and the Right Side," in *Lyrical and Critical Essays*, 17.

20. Albert Camus, "Nuptials at Tipasa," in *Lyrical and Critical Essays*, 69.

21. Albert Camus, "Death in the Soul," in *Lyrical and Critical Essays*, 49.

Chapter 9

1. *Notebooks 1935–1942*, 179.

Chapter 10

1. *Carnets I*, 173 (translation mine).

2. *Notebooks 1942–1951*, 264.

3. Quoted in McCarthy, *Camus*, 294.

4. *Notebooks 1935–1942*, 206.

5. Albert Camus, "Réflexions sur la guillotine" (Reflections on the Guillotine), in *Essais*, 1064 (translation mine).

6. Albert Camus, *Resistance, Rebellion, and Death*, trans. Justin O'Brien (New York: Knopf, 1961), 176–77.

7. Albert Camus, "Première Réponse," in *Essais*, 355–356.

8. Orwell, *Essays*, 174.

9. Camus, *The Rebel*, 283.

10. Orwell, *Essays*, 320.

11. Albert Camus, "*On a Philosophy of Expression* by Brice Parain," in *Lyrical and Critical Essays*, 238.

12. Orwell, *Essays*, 320.

Chapter 11

1. *Myth of Sisyphus*, 3.

2. *Notebooks 1942–1951*, 52.

Chapter 12

1. Quoted in O'Nan, "Biographical Context," 108.

2. *Exile and the Kingdom*, 109.

3. Sontag, *Against Interpretation*, 53.

4. Albert Camus, "Replies to Jean-Claude Brisville," in *Lyrical and Critical Essays*, 361.

5. Ibid., 362.

6. *Notebooks 1942–1951*, 249.

7. Brée, *Camus*, 86.

8. Albert Camus, "The Desert," in *Lyrical and Critical Essays*, 101.

9. *Notebooks 1935–1942*, 133–134.

Chapter 13

1. Albert Camus, "Discours de Suède: Commentaires," in *Essais*, 1892 (translation mine).

2. Albert Camus, "A Short Guide to Towns without a Past," in *Lyrical and Critical Essays*, 145.

3. *Notebooks 1935–1942*, 159.

4. *Notebooks 1942–1951*, 38.

5. Jean Grenier, *Albert Camus: Soleil et ombre: Une biographie intellectuale* (Albert Camus: Sun and Shade: An Intellectual Biography) (Paris: Gallimard, 1987), 155.

6. *Notebooks 1942–1951*, 51.

Chapter 14

1. Book 8, no. 7, letter to Socrates, [May or June] 1349, in Francesco Petrarca, *Rerum familiarium* (Familiar Things), (books 1–8, trans. Aldo S. Bernardo (Albany: State University of New York Press, 1975), 417.

2. *The Rebel*, 31.

3. Albert Camus, "Herman Melville," in *Lyrical and Critical Essays*, 289.

4. Camus, letter to Barthes, 11 January 1955, in *Lyrical and Critical Essays*, 339.

5. *Notebooks 1942–1951*, 53–54.

6. Randy Shilts, *And the Band Played on: Politics, People, and the AIDS Epidemic* (New York: St. Martin's, 1987), 18.

Notes and References

7. Ibid., 49.

8. Ibid., 34–35.

9. Stefan Kanfer, *A Journal of the Plague Years* (New York: Atheneum, 1973).

10. *Notebooks 1942–1951*, 28.

11. Archibald MacLeish, "Ars Poetica," in *Collected Poems 1917–1982* (Boston: Houghton Mifflin, 1985), 106.

12. Edgar Allan Poe, "The Poetic Principle," in *Edgar Allan Poe Essays and Reviews* (New York: The Library of America 1984), 75.

13. Charles Baudelaire, "The Didactic Heresy," in *The Modern Tradition: Backgrounds of Modern Literature*, ed. and trans. Richard Ellmann and Charles Feidelson, Jr. (New York: Oxford University Press, 1965), 101.

14. Oscar Wilde, *The Picture of Dorian Gray*, (in *Oscar Wilde*, ed. Isobel Murray. New York: Oxford University Press, 1989), 48.

15. Attributed to Samuel Goldwyn, perhaps apocryphal, in Michael Medved, *Hollywood vs. America: Popular Culture and the War on Traditional Values* (New York: HarperCollins, 1992), 307.

16. Orville Prescott, "Outstanding Novels," *Yale Review* 38 (Autumn 1948): 189.

17. Stephen Spender, *"Albert Camus, Citizen of the World" New York Times Book Review*, (1 August 1948): 1.

18. Milton Rugoff, *"New York Herald Tribune Weekly Book Review,"* (1 August 1948): 1.

19. *Myth of Sisyphus*, 101.

20. Ibid., 116.

21. Susan Sontag, *Illness as Metaphor* (New York: Farrar, Straus & Giroux, 1978), 3.

22. Ibid., 4.

23. *The Rebel*, 290.

24. *Notebooks 1942–1951*, 24.

25. *Notebooks 1935–1942*, 205.

26. Ibid., 193.

27. *Notebooks 1942–1951*, 51.

28. George Lukacs, *Realism in Our Time*, trans. John and Necke Mander (New York: Harper & Row, 1971), 59.

29. Lazere, *Unique Creation of Camus*, 176.

BIBLIOGRAPHY

Primary Works

Collected Editions in French

Théâtre, récits, nouvelles (Theater, Narratives, Stories). Edited by Roger Quilliot. Paris: Gallimard, Bibliothèque de la Pléiade; 1962. Authoritative edition of Camus's fiction, drama, and adaptations, including introductions, notes, variants, and complementary texts.

Carnets (Notebooks) I (1935–1942). Paris: Gallimard, 1962. Notebook entries from the earliest stages of composition of *La Peste*.

Carnets (Notebooks) II (1942–1951). Paris: Gallimard, 1964. Notebook observations during the writing, publication, and reception of *La Peste*.

Ecrits de jeunesse (Youthful Writings). Edited by Paul Viallaneix. Paris: Gallimard, 1973. Early writings, many published only posthumously.

Essais (Essays). Edited by Roger Quilliot and L. Faucon. Paris: Gallimard, Bibliothèque de La Pléiade; 1965. Authoritative edition of Camus's nonfiction prose, including introduction, notes, variants, and complementary texts.

La Mort heureuse (A Happy Death). Edited by Jean Sarocchi. Paris: Gallimard, 1971. Posthumously published, abandoned first novel, a forerunner of *The Stranger*.

Editions of *La Peste* in French

La Peste. Paris: Gallimard, 1947.

Bibliography

English Translations

Albert Camus: The Essential Writings. Edited by Robert E. Meagher. New York: Harper & Row, 1979.

Caligula and Three Other Plays. Translated by Stuart Gilbert. Paperback edition. New York: Vintage, 1962. Also includes *The Misunderstanding* (1944), *State of Siege* (1948), and *The Just Assassins* (1949).

Exile and the Kingdom. Translated by Justin O'Brien. Paperback edition. New York: Vintage, 1958. Includes "The Adulterous Woman," "The Renegade," "The Silent Men," "The Guest," "The Artist at Work," and "The Growing Stone."

The Fall. Translated by Justin O'Brien. Paperback edition. New York: Vintage, 1957.

The First Camus and Youthful Writings. Translated by Ellen Conroy Kennedy. New York: Knopf, 1976.

A Happy Death. Translated by Richard Howard. New York: Knopf, 1972. Posthumously published, a novel from which *The Stranger* evolved.

Lyrical and Critical Essays. Edited and with notes by Philip Thody. Translated by Ellen Conroy Kennedy. Paperback edition. New York: Vintage, 1970. Includes *The Wrong Side and the Right Side* (1937), *Nuptials* (1939), *Summer* (1954), as well as critical essays, letters, and interviews.

The Myth of Sisyphus and Other Essays. Translated by Justin O'Brien. New York: Knopf, 1955. Paperback edition. New York: Vintage, 1955. Includes *The Myth of Sisyphus* (1943), essays from *Nuptials* and *Summer*, and part of a 1953 interview.

Notebooks 1935–1942. Translated by Philip Thody. New York: Knopf, 1963.

Notebooks 1942–1951. Translated by Justin O'Brien. New York: Knopf, 1965.

The Plague. Translated by Stuart Gilbert. New York: Random House/Modern Library, 1948. The only published English translation, it is also available in a 1972 Vintage paperback with slightly different pagination.

The Rebel: An Essay on Man in Revolt. Translated by Anthony Bower. Foreword by Sir Herbert Read. Revised edition. New York: Knopf, 1978. First published 1954.

Resistance, Rebellion, and Death. Translated with an introduction by Justin O'Brien. New York: Knopf, 1961. Miscellaneous writings on capital punishment and other topics.

The Stranger. Translated by Stuart Gilbert. Paperback edition. New York: Knopf, 1946. Translated by Matthew Ward. New York: Vintage, 1989. The Vintage paperback is a more recent, Americanized translation. Paperback edition.

117

Secondary Works

Bibliographies

Gay-Crosier, Raymond, ed. "Camus." In *The Twentieth Century*, ed. Douglas W. Alden and Richard A. Brooks. pt. 3, chap. 34, pp. 1573–1679, nos. 14426–15572. In *A Critical Bibliography of French Literature*, vol. 6, ed. David Clark Cabeen. Syracuse: Syracuse University Press, 1980. Classified and annotated list of works on Camus.

Hoy, Peter C. *Camus in English: An Annotated Bibliography of Albert Camus's Contribution to English and American Periodicals and Newspapers*. Second edition. Paris: Lettres Modernes, 1971.

MLA International Bibliography. New York: Modern Language Association, 1922–. Elaborate annual list of criticism and scholarship in modern languages and literatures. Format in recent years has provided more sophisticated indexing by theme as well as nationality and era. The data base of the bibliography is accessible on-line through DIALOG INFORMATION SERVICES and its subsidiary KNOWLEDGE INDEX.

Roeming, Robert F. *Camus: A Bibliography*. Seventh edition. Microfiche. Milwaukee: Computing Services of the University of Wisconsin, 1987. An updated inventory of works in many languages by and about Camus.

Books in English

Amoia, Alba. *Albert Camus*. New York: Continuum, 1989. A general introduction to Camus as an important "Mediterranean" figure. Its chapter on *The Plague* is subtitled "A Holograph."

Bloom Harold, ed. *Albert Camus: Modern Critical Views*. New York: Chelsea House, 1989. Introduction, chronology, and bibliography, as well as reprints of several varied essays on Camus.

Brée, Germaine. *Camus*. Revised edition. New York: Harcourt, Brace & World, 1964. An important retrospective of Camus's career, with emphasis on the literary works.

———. *Camus and Sartre: Crisis and Commitment*. New York: Delta, 1972. A partisan of Camus, Brée examines the complementary and colliding careers of two formidable comrades and rivals.

———, ed. *Camus: A Collection of Critical Essays*. Englewood Cliffs, N.J.: Prentice-Hall, 1962. Collects the most important essays on Camus written until immediately after his death.

Ellison, David R. *Understanding Albert Camus*. Columbia: University of South

Bibliography

Carolina Press, 1990. For nonspecialist readers, an introductory overview of the career that integrates philosophical with literary writings.

Fitch, Brian T. *The Narcissistic Text: A Reading of Camus' Fiction.* Toronto: University of Toronto Press, 1982. Sophisticated study of Camus as metafictionalist. Separate chapter on *The Plague.*

Haggis, D. R. *Albert Camus: La Peste.* London: Edward Arnold, 1962. A brief introduction to Camus's life and times and the genesis, imagery, structure, and style of *The Plague.*

Kellman, Steven G., ed. *Approaches to Teaching Camus's "The Plague."* New York: Modern Language Association, 1985. Fourteen professors from a variety of disciplines discuss *The Plague* as a classroom text. Also includes useful bibliographical survey.

Knapp, Bettina L., ed. *Critical Essays on Albert Camus.* Boston: G. K. Hall, 1988. Ten newly commissioned essays [out of a total of 14] from a variety of perspectives on the life and works of Camus.

Lazere, Donald. *The Unique Creation of Albert Camus.* New Haven: Yale University Press, 1973. An argument for the unity, even circularity, of Camus's corpus, it emphasizes his ties to American authors and readers.

Lottman, Herbert R. *Albert Camus: A Biography.* Garden City, N.Y.: Doubleday, 1979. Assiduously researched, the most thorough study of the author's life.

McCarthy, Patrick. *Camus.* New York: Random House, 1982. Intended for the nonspecialist general reader, this biography is particularly attentive to Camus's North African identity.

Merton, Thomas. *Albert Camus's "The Plague": Introduction and Commentary.* New York: Seabury, 1968. A personal reading of Camus's novel by a renowned theologian.

O'Brien, Conor Cruise. *Albert Camus of Europe and Africa.* New York: Viking, 1970. A political discussion of Camus that is often perceptive and often hostile.

Parker, Emmett. *Albert Camus: The Artist in the Arena.* Madison: University of Wisconsin Press, 1966. Traces the evolution of Camus's thought, through his journalism and polemics as well as his fiction, with particular attention to the tension he felt between art and political commitment.

Quilliot, Roger. *The Sea and Prisons: A Commentary on the Life and Thought of Albert Camus.* Translated by Emmett Parker. University: University of Alabama Press, 1970. A revised study of the contradictory career of Camus, by a French scholar who knew him.

Rhein, Phillip H. *Albert Camus.* New York: Twayne, Twayne World Authors Series, 1969. Useful overview of Camus's career.

Sprintzen, David. *Albert Camus: A Critical Examination.* Philadelphia: Temple University Press, 1988. A survey of Camus's career, with particular emphasis on his continuing cultural significance.

Tarrow, Susan. *Exile from the Kingdom: A Political Rereading of Albert Camus.* University: University of Alabama Press, 1985. A rereading, in chronological order, of Camus's journalism and fiction as linked to historical events and as embodiment of his political ambivalences. A chapter on *The Plague* is subtitled "A Totalitarian Universe."

Thody, Philip. *Albert Camus, 1913–1960.* New York: Macmillan, 1962. Traces Camus's embattled career and thought and, in a separate chapter on *The Plague*, praises the novel for its ambitions and accessibility.

Books in French

Albert Camus, 8, "Camus Romancier: *La Peste*" (Camus the Novelist: *The Plague*) (1976). One issue in an irregular journal series on Camus, published, entirely in French, through *La Revue des lettres modernes*. Each volume contains a variety of articles and a review of recent scholarship. From 1968 to 1988, edited by Brian T. Fitch, since 1989 by Raymond Gay-Crosier.

Bartfield, Fernarde. *L'Effet tragique: Essai sur le tragique dans l'oeuvre de Camus.* (The Tragic Effect: Essay on the Tragic in the Work of Camus). Geneva: Slatkine, 1988. An attempt to define the tragic and apply it to the work of Camus.

Crochet, Monique. *Les Mythes dans l'oeuvre de Camus* (Myths in the Work of Camus). Paris: Editions Universitaires, 1973. Myths in Camus's work, including Sisyphus, Orpheus, Don Juan, and the plague itself.

Fortier, Paul A. *Une Lecture de Camus: La valeur des éléments descriptifs dans l'oeuvre romanesque.* (A Reading of Camus, the Value of Descriptive Elements in His Novelistic Work). Paris: Editions Klincksieck, 1977. Analysis of how Camus creates his emotional and geographical landscapes.

Gaillard, Pol. *La Peste Camus: Analyse critique* (*The Plague* of Camus: Critical Analysis). Paris: Hatier, 1972. A brief, intelligent introduction to the themes, characters, structure, and style of Camus's novel.

Gassin, Jean. *L'Univers symbolique d'Albert Camus: Essai d'interprétation psychanalytique.* (The Symbolic Universe of Albert Camus: A Psychoanalytic Interpretation). Paris: Minard, 1981. Psychoanalytic interpretation of recurrent symbols in Camus's works.

Grenier, Jean. *Albert Camus: Souvenirs* (Albert Camus: Remembrances). Paris: Gallimard, 1968. Memoirs of Camus's Algerian mentor and an important Francophonic author in his own right.

Bibliography

————. *Albert Camus: Soleil et ombre: Une biographie intellectuelle* (Albert Camus: Sun and Shade: An Intellectual Biography). Paris: Gallimard, 1987. Grenier's intellectual biography of Camus that stresses his distinctive artistic landscape.

Lenzini, José. *L'Algérie de Camus* (Camus's Algeria). Aix-en-Provence: Edisud, 1987. Study of Camus's native land and its importance to his writing.

Mailhot, Laurent. *Albert Camus, ou, L'Imagination du désert* (Albert Camus, or the Imagination of the Desert). Montreal: Presses de l'Université de Montréal, 1973. A thematic study of the function of landscape, particularly the desert, in the writings of Camus.

Mino, Hiroshi. *Le Silence dans l'oeuvre d'Albert Camus* (Silence in the Works of Albert Camus). Paris: Corti, 1987. Analysis of silence as theme and structural principle in Camus's writings.

Reichelberg, Ruth. *Albert Camus: Une Approche du sacré* (Albert Camus: An Approach to the Sacred). Paris: Nizet, 1983. The theme of the sacred in Camus's career.

Roy, Jules. *A propos d'Alger, de Camus et du hasard* (Concerning Algiers, Camus, and Chance). Pezennas: Haut Quartier, 1982. Another Francophonic North African author's salute to Camus, Algiers, and Algeria.

Articles and Chapters in Books in English

Barnett, Richard L. "Nothing but Difference: Of Poetic Rescission in Camus's *La Peste*." *Symposium* 41 (Fall 1987): 163–73. A semiotic reading that argues that the novel deconstructs itself.

Bertocci, Angelo. "Camus's *La Peste* and the Absurd." *Romanic Review* 49 (February 1958): 33–41. Early English-language attempt to situate Camus's novel within the context of existential philosophy.

Cohn, Robert Greer. "The True Camus." *French Review* 60, no. 1 (October 1986): 30–38. An admiring reevaluation of Camus's achievement.

Cruickshank, John. "The Art of Allegory in *La Peste*." *Symposium* 9 (Spring 1957): 61–74. Analyzes the inappropriateness of the plague as representation of the Nazi Occupation.

Finel-Honigman, Irène. "Oran: Protagonist, Myth, and Allegory." *Modern Fiction Studies* 24 (Spring 1977): 75–81. The Algerian city as transformed into the setting for *The Plague*.

————. "The Orpheus and Eurydice Myth in Camus's *The Plague*." *Classical and Modern Literature* 1 (1983): 207–18. Traces Camus's use of Orpheus and Eurydice to Virgil's *Fourth Georgic*.

Greene, Robert W. "Fluency, Muteness, and Commitment in Camus's *La Peste*." *French Studies* 34 (October 1980): 422–33.

Grobe, Edwin P. "Camus and the Parable of the Perfect Sentence." *Symposium* 24 (Fall 1970): 254–61. A suggestive study of Joseph Grand and his literary ambitions.

———. "Tarrou's Confession: The Ethical Force of the Past Definite." *French Review* 39 (February 1965): 550–58. Finds in Jean Tarrou's recollections to Rieux a transition from adolescent to adult consciousness.

Hollahan, Eugene. "The Path of Sympathy: Abstraction and Imagination in Camus's *La Peste*." *Studies in the Novel* 8 (Winter 1976): 377–93.

Kellman, Steven G. "Singular Third Person: Camus' *La Peste*." *Kentucky Romance Quarterly* 25 no. 4 (1978): 499–507. A study of the peculiar narrative strategy of Rieux's chronicle.

———. "*La Peste*: Infected By the Bacillus of Self-Consciousness." *L'Esprit Créateur* (Summer 1991): 22–29. A study of Camus's novel as a work of metafiction.

Moses, Edwin. "Functional Complexity: The Narrative Techniques of *The Plague*." *Modern Fiction Studies* 20 (Autumn 1974): 419–29. The logistics of Rieux' narration.

O'Nan, Martha, "Biographical Context and Its Importance to Classroom Study." In Kellman, *"Approaches to Teaching Camus's "The Plague,"* 102–9.

Place, D. S. "Character in Camus' *La Peste*." *Modern Languages* 69 (1988): 96–100.

Porter, Laurence M. "From Chronicle to Novel: Artistic Elaboration in Camus's *La Peste*." *Modern Fiction Studies* 28 (Winter 1982–83): 589–96. Rieux's chronicle examined in relationship to history and language.

Rizzuto, Anthony. "Camus and a Society without Women." *Modern Language Studies* 13 (Winter 1983): 3–14. Examination of misogyny, procreation, and the role of women in Camus's works and life.

Stephanson, Raymond. "The Plague Narratives of Defoe and Camus: Illness as Metaphor." *Modern Language Quarterly* 48 (September 1987): 224–41. Epidemics and the imagination in *Journal of the Plague Year* and *The Plague*.

Sterling, Elwyn F. "Albert Camus' *La Peste*: Cottard's Act of Madness." *College Literature* 13 (Spring 1986): 177–85. Discusses Cottard in relationship to the human condition, evil, and morality.

Zants, Emily. "Relationship of Judge and Priest in *La Peste*." *French Review* (February 1964): 419–25. Argues that Camus refuses to accept a distinction between temporal justice and religion's concern with the eternal.

Zimmerman, Eugenia N. "*The Plague and Its Contracts*." In Kellman, *Approaches to Teaching Camus's "The Plague,"* 54–62.

Bibliography

Articles and Chapters in Books in French

Barilli, Renato. "Camus et le Nouveau Roman." (Camus and the New Novel). In *Albert Camus: Oeuvre fermée, oeuvre ouverte?* (Albert Camus: Closed Work, Open Work?) ed. Raymond Gay-Crosier and Jacqueline Lévi-Valensi, 201–14. Paris: Gallimard, 1985. Discussion of Camus's relationship to the "new novelists" of the 1950s and 1960s.

Inada, Harutoshi. "Comment raconter son propre malheur? La Dialectique de l'individual et du général dans *La Peste.*" (How to Recount One's Own Misfortune? The Dialectic of the Individual and the General in *The Plague*). *Etudes de Langues et Littératures Françaises* 52 (March 1988): 159–76. Analysis of how the narrative treats individual character and experience.

Lévi-Valensi, Jacqueline. "Le temps et l'espace dans l'oeuvre romanesque de Camus: Une mythologie du réel." (Time and Space in the Novelistic Work of Camus: A Mythology of the Real) In *Albert Camus 1980*, ed. Raymond Gay-Crosier, 57–68. Gainesville: University Presses of Florida, 1980. Analysis of how Camus reconceives space and time in his novels.

Poirot-Delpech, Bertrand. "Justice pour Camus." (Justice for Camus). *Le Monde*, 5 August 1977. An influential, journalistic attempt to resuscitate Camus's reputation by arguing that he was ahead of his time.

Index

Index

THE AUTHOR

Steven G. Kellman received his doctorate in comparative literature from the University of California at Berkeley in 1972. He has taught at Bemidji State Minnesota, Tel-Aviv University, the University of California at Irvine, the University of California at Berkeley, and the University of Texas at San Antonio, where he is currently professor of comparative literature. He has served as a Fulbright lecturer in the Soviet Union and a Partners of the Americas lecturer in Peru. He is the editor of *Approaches to Teaching Camus's "The Plague,"* published by the Modern Language Association in 1985, as well as the author of many articles on Camus and other twentieth-century novelists. His other books include *The Self-Begetting Novel* (1980), *Loving Reading: Erotics of the Text* (1985), and *The Modern American Novel* (1991). Kellman is fiction critic for the *Gettysburg Review* and film critic for the *Texas Observer*. His column for the *San Antonio Light* received the 1986 H. L. Mencken Award.